# RYA Day Skipper Shorebased Notes

e Lucas

www.rya.org.uk

© RYA
This edition published 2014
**The Royal Yachting Association**
RYA House, Ensign Way,
Hamble, Southampton,
Hampshire SO31 4YA

**Tel:** 0844 556 9555
**Fax:** 0844 556 9516
**E-mail:** publications@rya.org.uk
**Web:** www.rya.org.uk
Follow us on Twitter @RYAPublications
or on YouTube
**ISBN:** 978-1-906435912
**RYA Order Code:** DSN

All rights reserved. No part of this publication may be reproduced, stored in a retrieval system, or transmitted, in any form or by any means, electronic, mechanical, photocopying, recording or otherwise, without prior permission in writing from the publishers.

A CIP record of this book is available from the British Library
Note: While all reasonable care has been taken in the preparation of this book, the publisher takes no responsibility for the use of the methods or products or contracts described in this book.

**Cover design:** Pete Galvin
**Acknowledgements:** Penny Haire, Sara Hopkinson, Simon Jinks
**Typeset:** Creativebyte
**Proofreading:** Rob Melotti
Printed in China by World Print Ltd

*Totally Chlorine Free*
*Sustainable Forests*

# Contents

| | | | |
|---|---|---|---|
| Nautical Terms | 3 | Chart Features | 66 |
| Typical Sailing Yacht | 4 | Interpreting Charts | 68 |
| Typical Motor Cruiser | 8 | Plotting your Position | 70 |
| Sailing Theory | 10 | Variation | 74 |
| Stability | 12 | Deviation | 76 |
| Types of Sailing Yacht | 16 | Tidal Theory | 78 |
| Types of Motor Vessel | 18 | Tidal Streams | 87 |
| Knots | 24 | Dead Reckoning Position | 90 |
| Ropework | 26 | Estimated Position | 91 |
| Mooring Alongside | 28 | Course to Steer | 92 |
| Anchoring | 33 | Fixing your Position | 96 |
| Safety Equipment | 38 | Waypoints | 100 |
| Personal Safety and Comfort | 40 | Buoyage | 104 |
| Fire Safety | 44 | Lights | 109 |
| Fire Fighting | 46 | Pilotage | 111 |
| Emergency Procedures | 48 | Making and Following a Pilotage Plan | 116 |
| Cold Shock | 49 | Weather Systems | 118 |
| Emergency Services | 50 | Weather Forecasts | 120 |
| Raising the Alarm | 52 | Land and Sea Breezes | 122 |
| Rules of the Road | 56 | Weather and Passage Making | 123 |
| Lights and Shapes | 60 | Beaufort Wind Scale | 125 |

The skills required to skipper a boat safely, navigate from port to port and moor up at the end of the day are the same the world over. However, there are two notable differences that can catch out the unwary when sailing in different parts of the world; the circulation of weather patterns in the Northern and Southern Hemispheres and the layout of buoyage in the Eastern and Western Hemispheres. Both of these differences are covered in the book, but ensure you use the correct system for your sailing area.

Charts reproduced throughout this book are for training purposes only. On no account should they be used for navigation.

# Nautical Terms

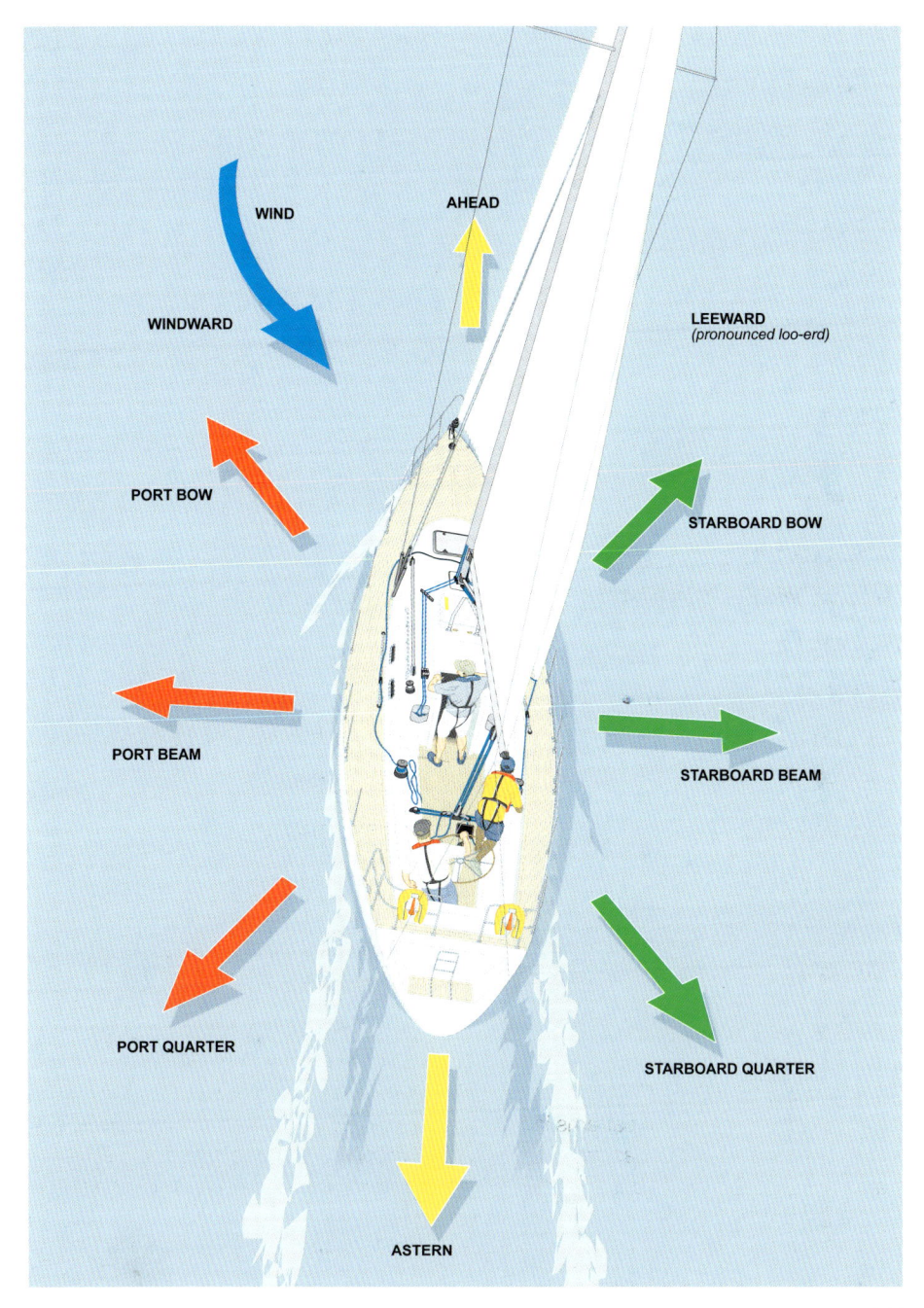

## Typical Sailing Yacht

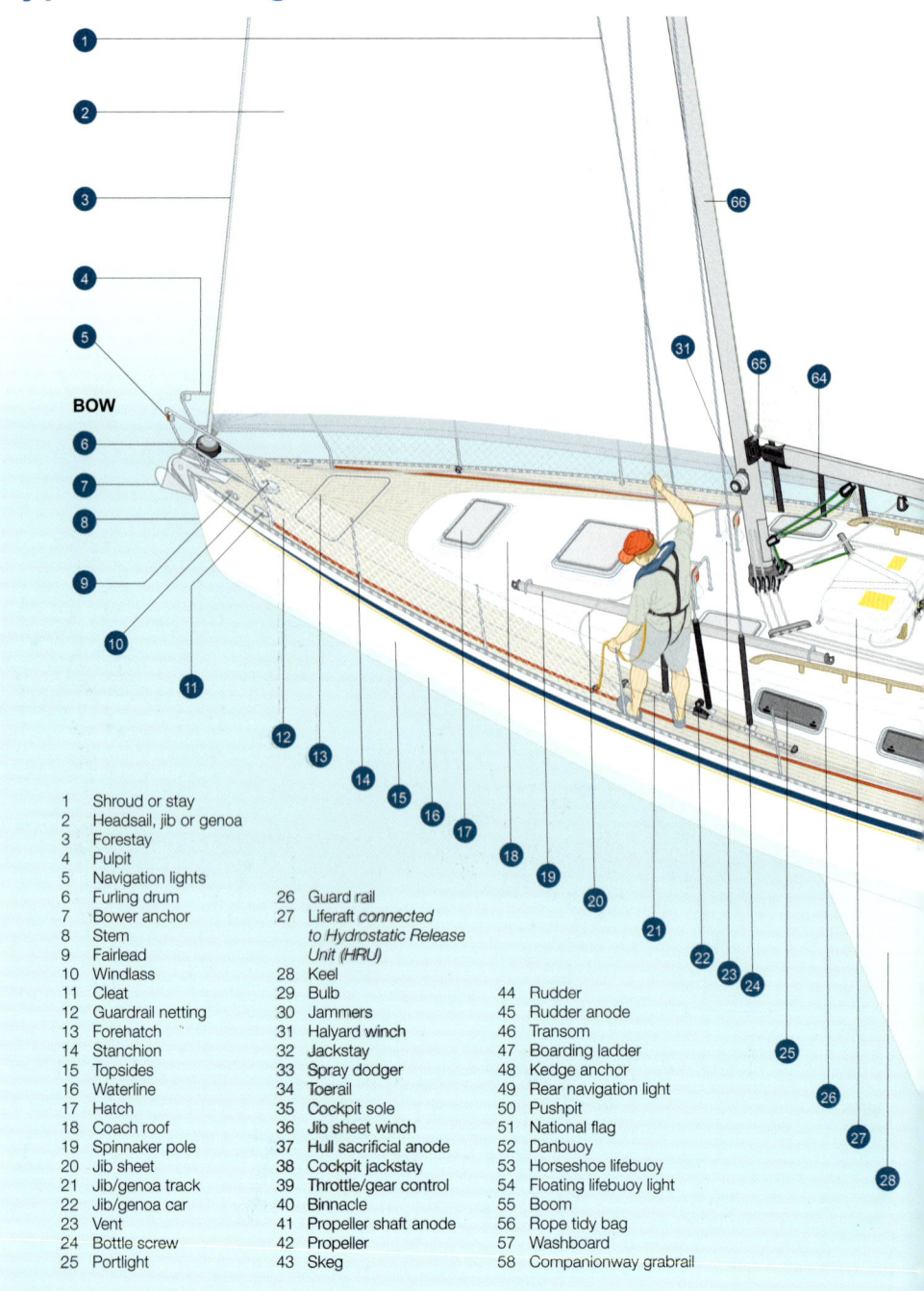

**BOW**

| # | Label | # | Label | # | Label |
|---|---|---|---|---|---|
| 1 | Shroud or stay | | | | |
| 2 | Headsail, jib or genoa | | | | |
| 3 | Forestay | | | | |
| 4 | Pulpit | | | | |
| 5 | Navigation lights | | | | |
| 6 | Furling drum | 26 | Guard rail | | |
| 7 | Bower anchor | 27 | Liferaft *connected to Hydrostatic Release Unit (HRU)* | | |
| 8 | Stem | | | | |
| 9 | Fairlead | | | | |
| 10 | Windlass | 28 | Keel | | |
| 11 | Cleat | 29 | Bulb | 44 | Rudder |
| 12 | Guardrail netting | 30 | Jammers | 45 | Rudder anode |
| 13 | Forehatch | 31 | Halyard winch | 46 | Transom |
| 14 | Stanchion | 32 | Jackstay | 47 | Boarding ladder |
| 15 | Topsides | 33 | Spray dodger | 48 | Kedge anchor |
| 16 | Waterline | 34 | Toerail | 49 | Rear navigation light |
| 17 | Hatch | 35 | Cockpit sole | 50 | Pushpit |
| 18 | Coach roof | 36 | Jib sheet winch | 51 | National flag |
| 19 | Spinnaker pole | 37 | Hull sacrificial anode | 52 | Danbuoy |
| 20 | Jib sheet | 38 | Cockpit jackstay | 53 | Horseshoe lifebuoy |
| 21 | Jib/genoa track | 39 | Throttle/gear control | 54 | Floating lifebuoy light |
| 22 | Jib/genoa car | 40 | Binnacle | 55 | Boom |
| 23 | Vent | 41 | Propeller shaft anode | 56 | Rope tidy bag |
| 24 | Bottle screw | 42 | Propeller | 57 | Washboard |
| 25 | Portlight | 43 | Skeg | 58 | Companionway grabrail |

[ 4 ]

Typical Sailing Yacht

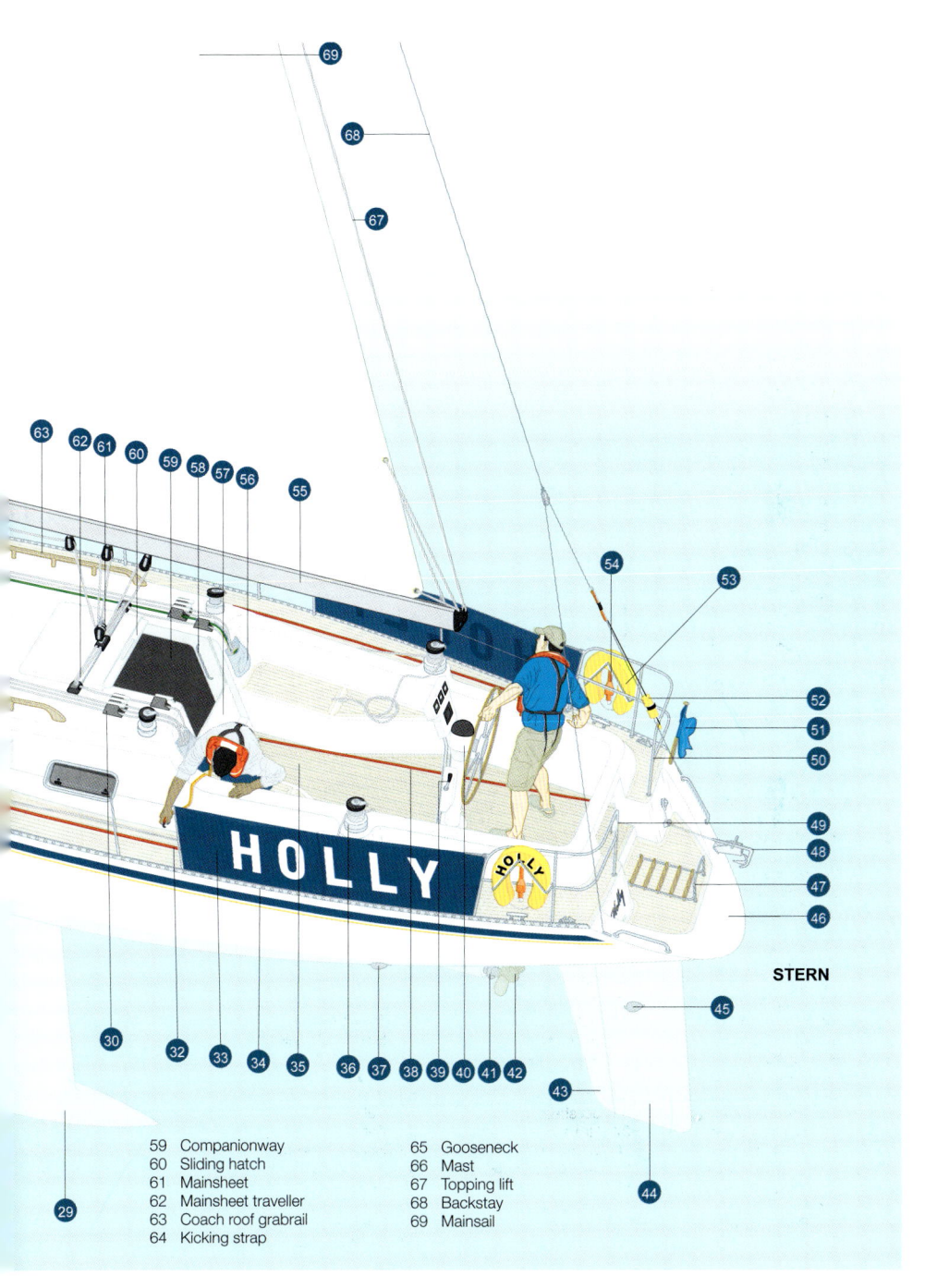

59 Companionway
60 Sliding hatch
61 Mainsheet
62 Mainsheet traveller
63 Coach roof grabrail
64 Kicking strap
65 Gooseneck
66 Mast
67 Topping lift
68 Backstay
69 Mainsail

**STERN**

[ 5 ]

Typical Sailing Yacht

## BELOW DECK

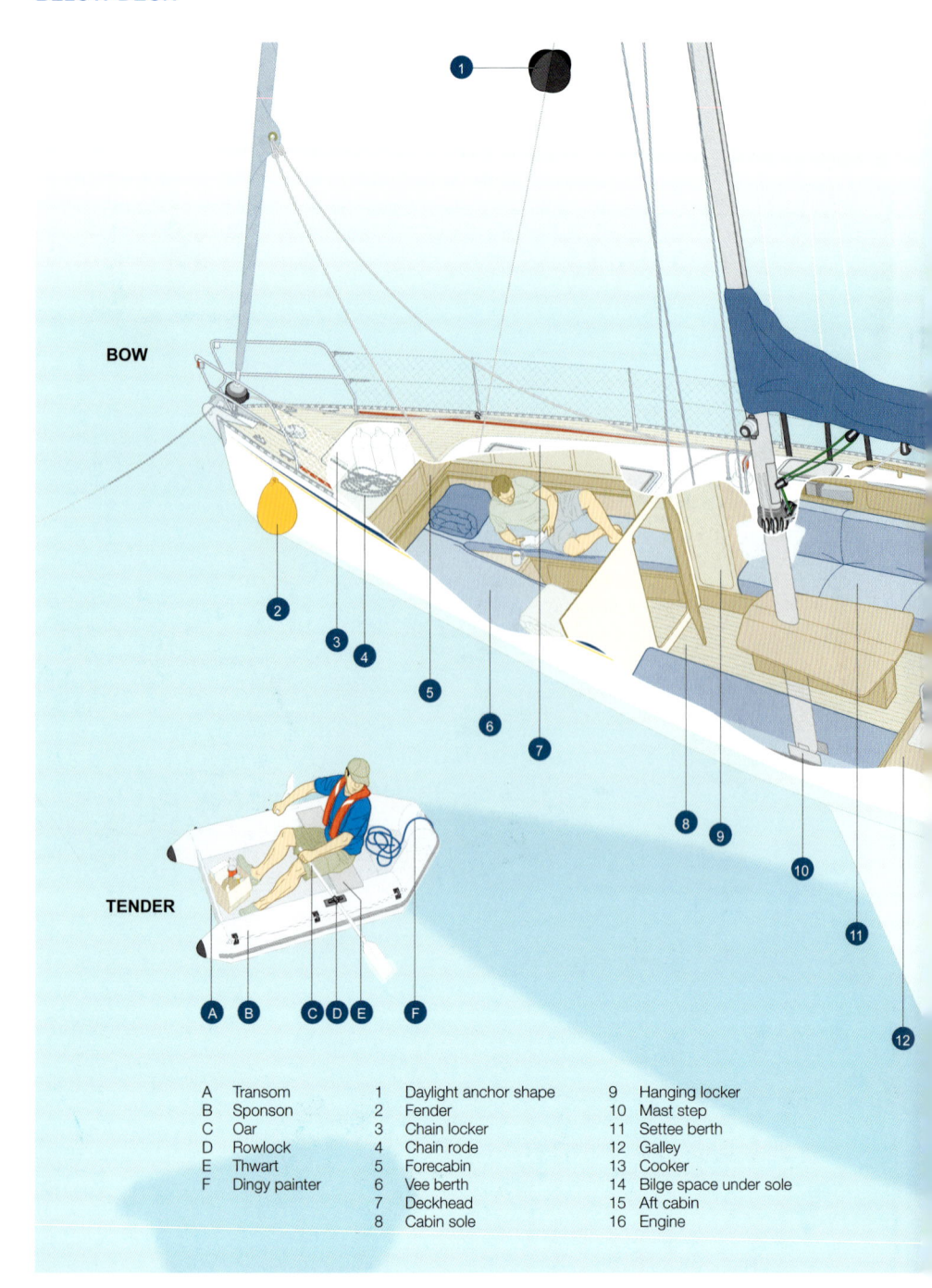

**BOW**

**TENDER**

| A | Transom | 1 | Daylight anchor shape | 9 | Hanging locker |
| --- | --- | --- | --- | --- | --- |
| B | Sponson | 2 | Fender | 10 | Mast step |
| C | Oar | 3 | Chain locker | 11 | Settee berth |
| D | Rowlock | 4 | Chain rode | 12 | Galley |
| E | Thwart | 5 | Forecabin | 13 | Cooker |
| F | Dingy painter | 6 | Vee berth | 14 | Bilge space under sole |
| | | 7 | Deckhead | 15 | Aft cabin |
| | | 8 | Cabin sole | 16 | Engine |

Typical Sailing Yacht

**STERN**

17  Quarter berth
18  Head (toilet compartment)
19  Vented loop and skin fitting
20  Gas bottle locker
21  Coaming locker
22  VHF radio

23  Radar
24  Instruments GPS,
    depth sounder etc.
25  Plotting instruments
26  Plotting table

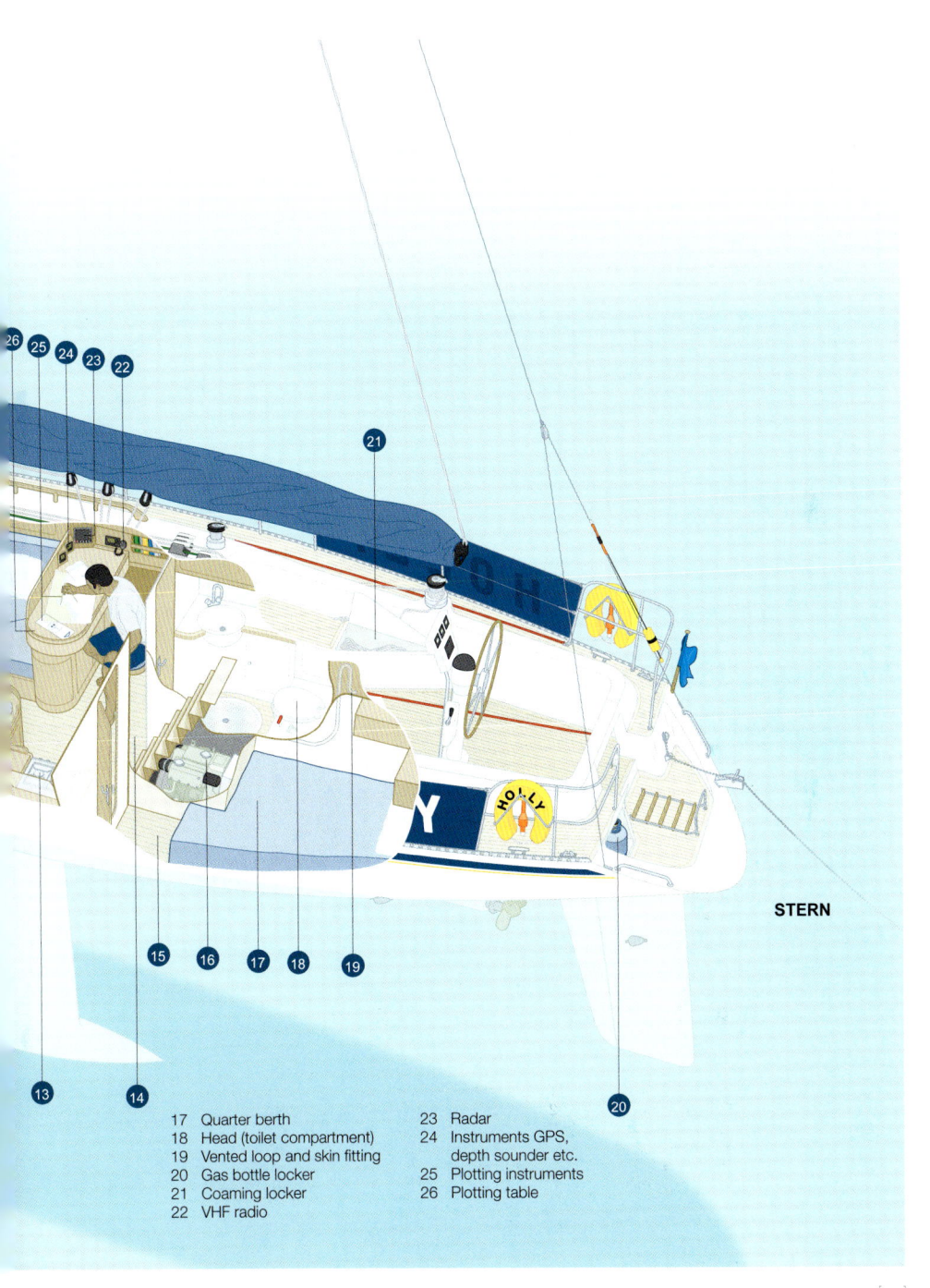

[ 7 ]

# Typical Motor Cruiser

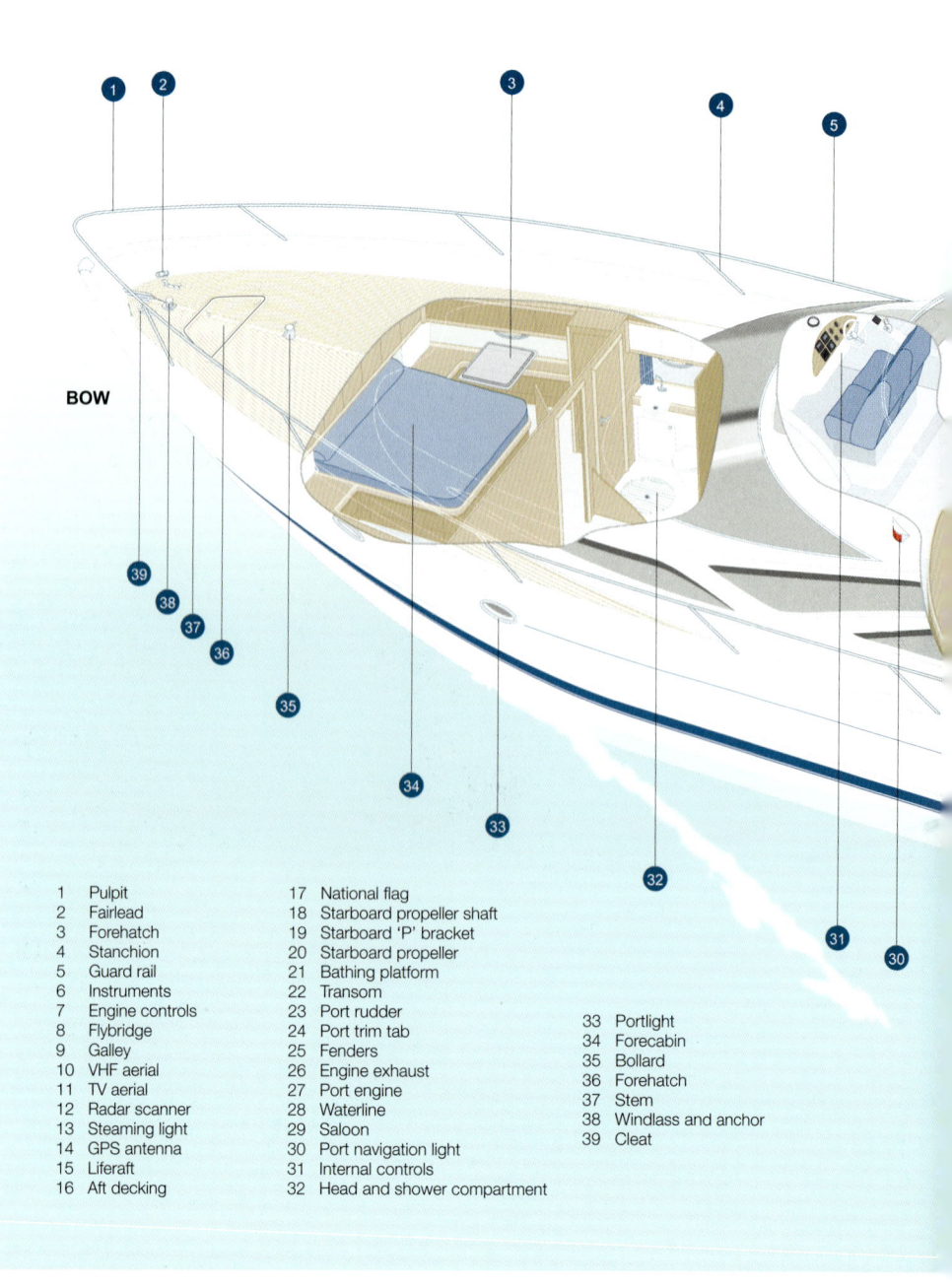

BOW

| | | | | | |
|---|---|---|---|---|---|
| 1 | Pulpit | 17 | National flag | | |
| 2 | Fairlead | 18 | Starboard propeller shaft | | |
| 3 | Forehatch | 19 | Starboard 'P' bracket | | |
| 4 | Stanchion | 20 | Starboard propeller | | |
| 5 | Guard rail | 21 | Bathing platform | | |
| 6 | Instruments | 22 | Transom | | |
| 7 | Engine controls | 23 | Port rudder | 33 | Portlight |
| 8 | Flybridge | 24 | Port trim tab | 34 | Forecabin |
| 9 | Galley | 25 | Fenders | 35 | Bollard |
| 10 | VHF aerial | 26 | Engine exhaust | 36 | Forehatch |
| 11 | TV aerial | 27 | Port engine | 37 | Stem |
| 12 | Radar scanner | 28 | Waterline | 38 | Windlass and anchor |
| 13 | Steaming light | 29 | Saloon | 39 | Cleat |
| 14 | GPS antenna | 30 | Port navigation light | | |
| 15 | Liferaft | 31 | Internal controls | | |
| 16 | Aft decking | 32 | Head and shower compartment | | |

Typical Motor Cruiser

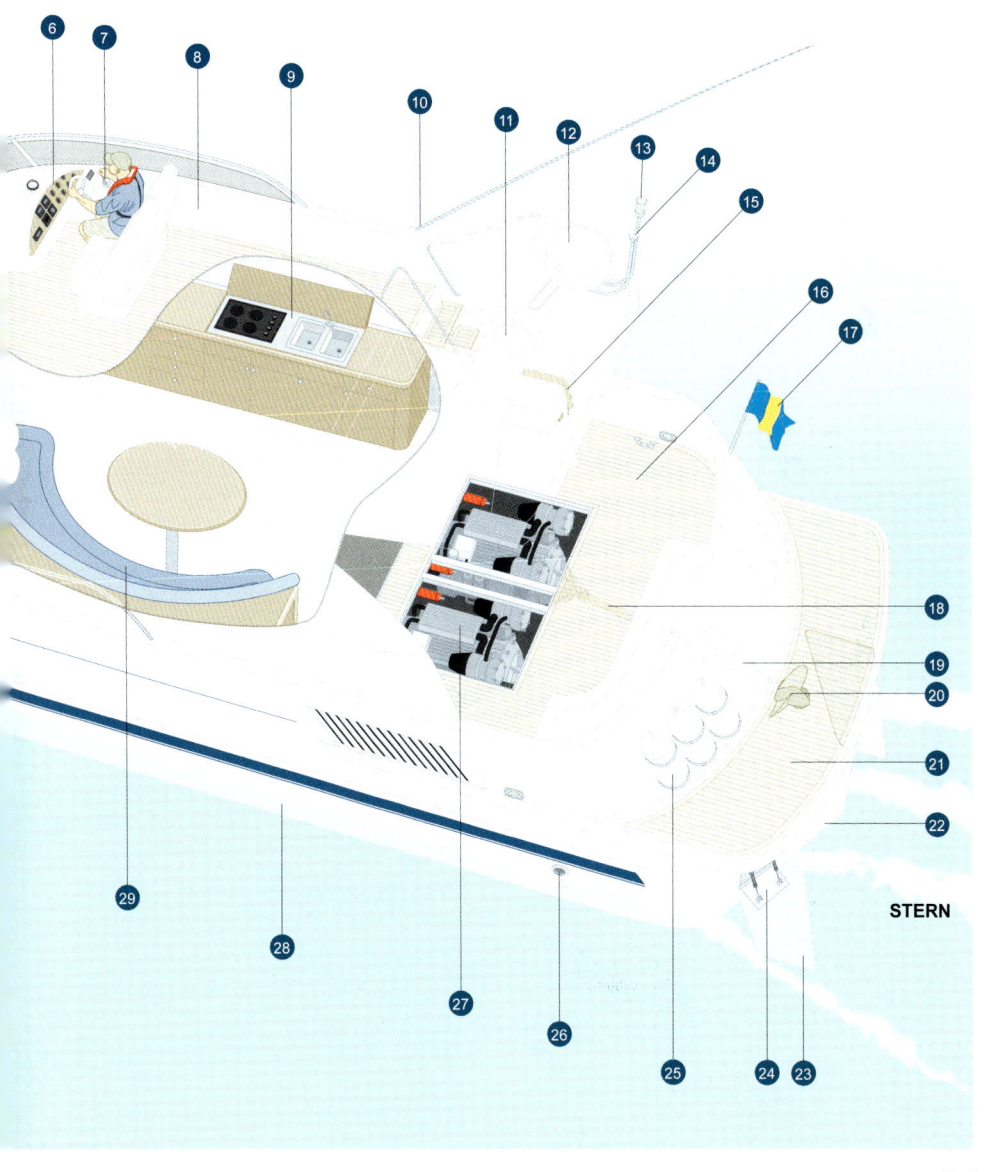

STERN

[ 9 ]

Sailing Theory

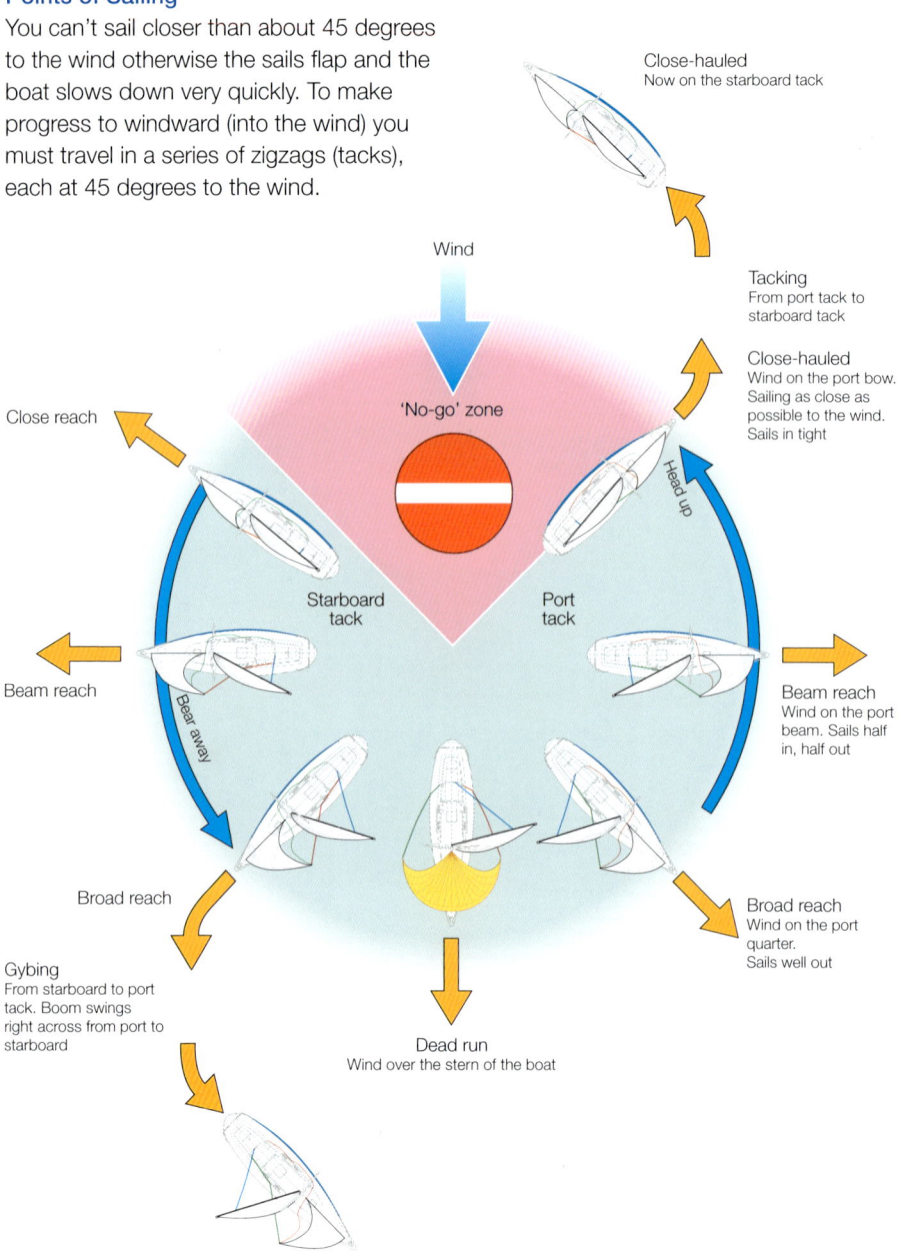

# Sailing Theory

## Points of Sailing
You can't sail closer than about 45 degrees to the wind otherwise the sails flap and the boat slows down very quickly. To make progress to windward (into the wind) you must travel in a series of zigzags (tacks), each at 45 degrees to the wind.

Wind

'No-go' zone

Starboard tack

Port tack

Head up

Bear away

Close reach

Beam reach

Broad reach

**Gybing**
From starboard to port tack. Boom swings right across from port to starboard

**Dead run**
Wind over the stern of the boat

**Close-hauled**
Now on the starboard tack

**Tacking**
From port tack to starboard tack

**Close-hauled**
Wind on the port bow. Sailing as close as possible to the wind. Sails in tight

**Beam reach**
Wind on the port beam. Sails half in, half out

**Broad reach**
Wind on the port quarter. Sails well out

[ 10 ]

Sailing Theory

## SIMPLE SAILING THEORY

When you put a spoon into running water it is sucked into the flow.

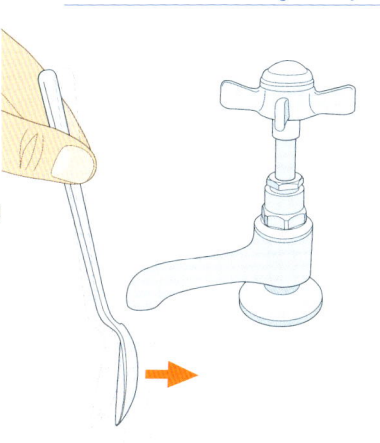

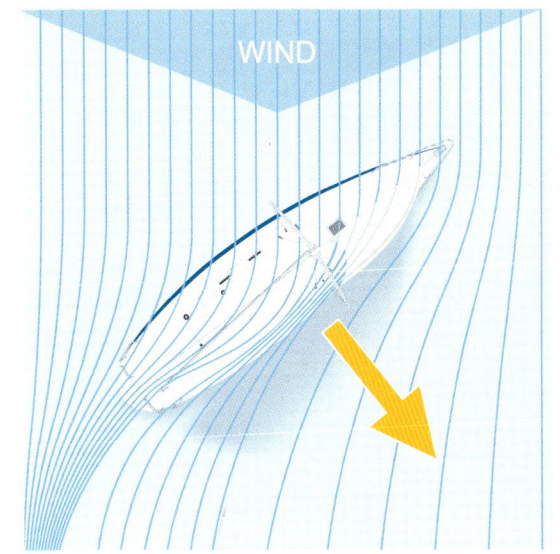

WIND

Similarly, when air flows over a sail it creates a sideways force.

A combination of sideways force from the sail and opposite resistance from the water pushes the boat forward, like squeezing a bar of wet soap.

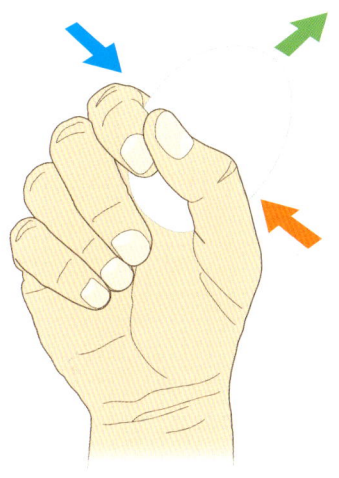

[ 11 ]

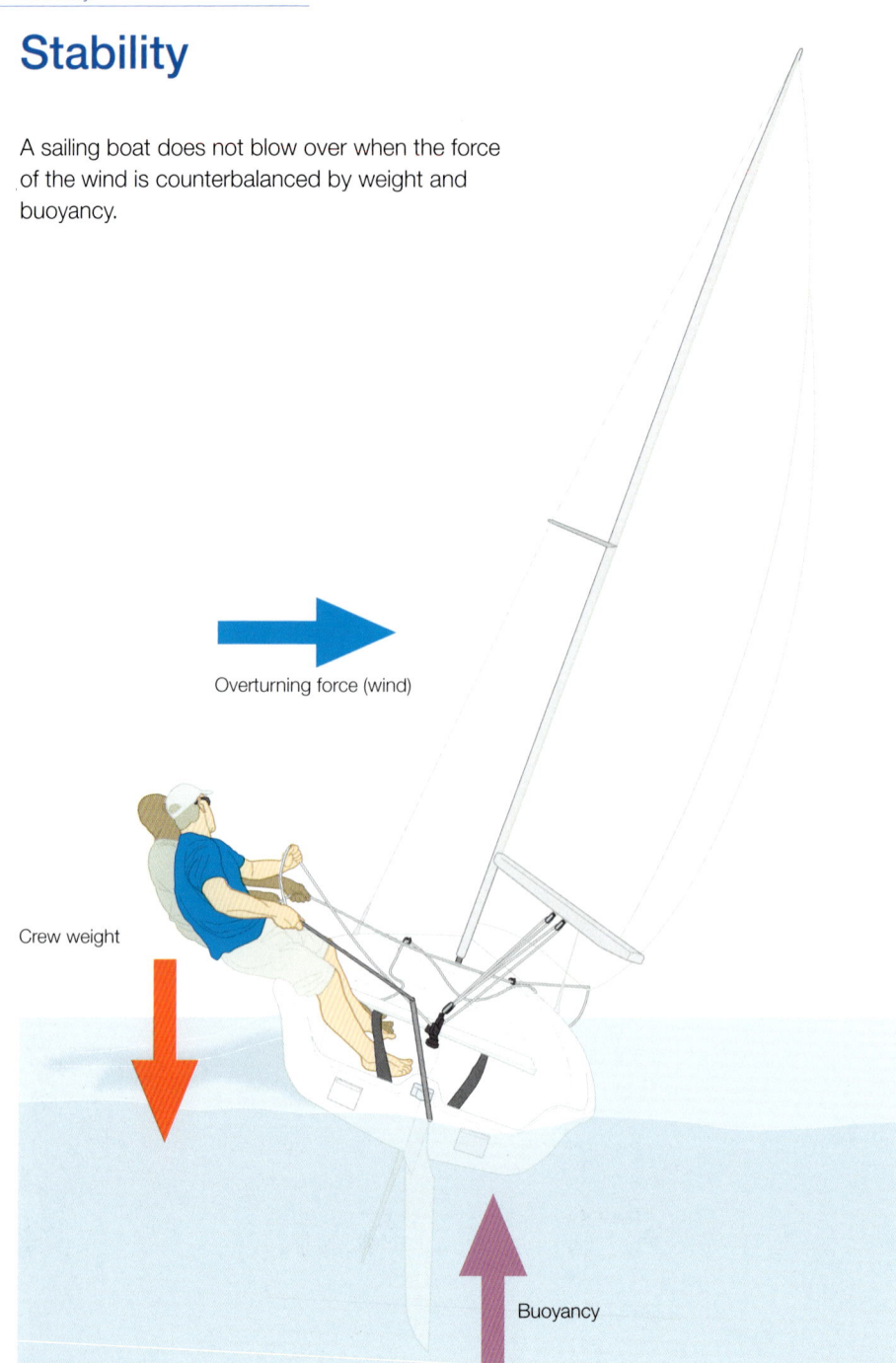

Stability

# Stability

A sailing boat does not blow over when the force of the wind is counterbalanced by weight and buoyancy.

Overturning force (wind)

Crew weight

Buoyancy

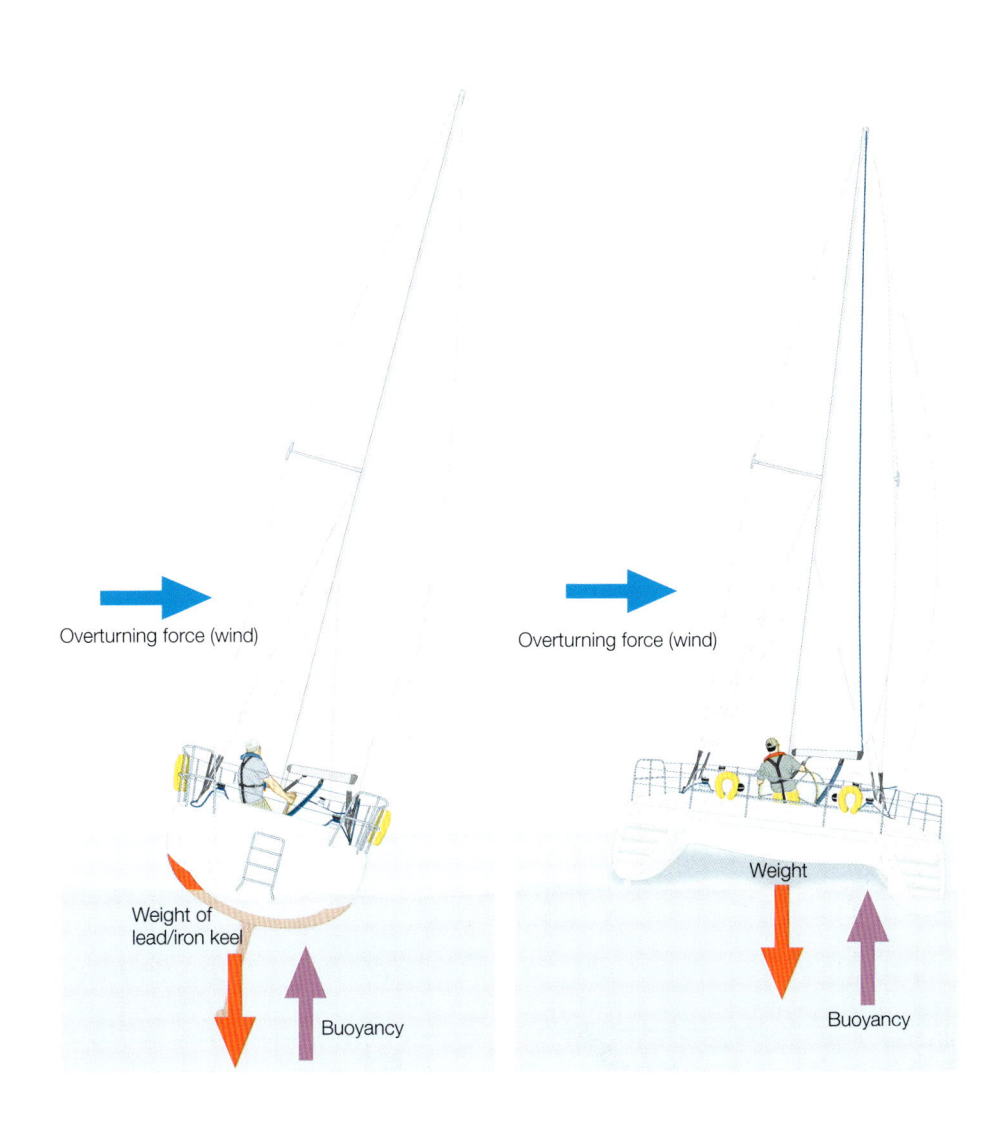

Stability

Overturning force (wind)

Overturning force (wind)

Weight of lead/iron keel

Buoyancy

Weight

Buoyancy

[ 13 ]

## Stability

These three stability curves are drawn to scale, assuming vessels of similar size and mass.

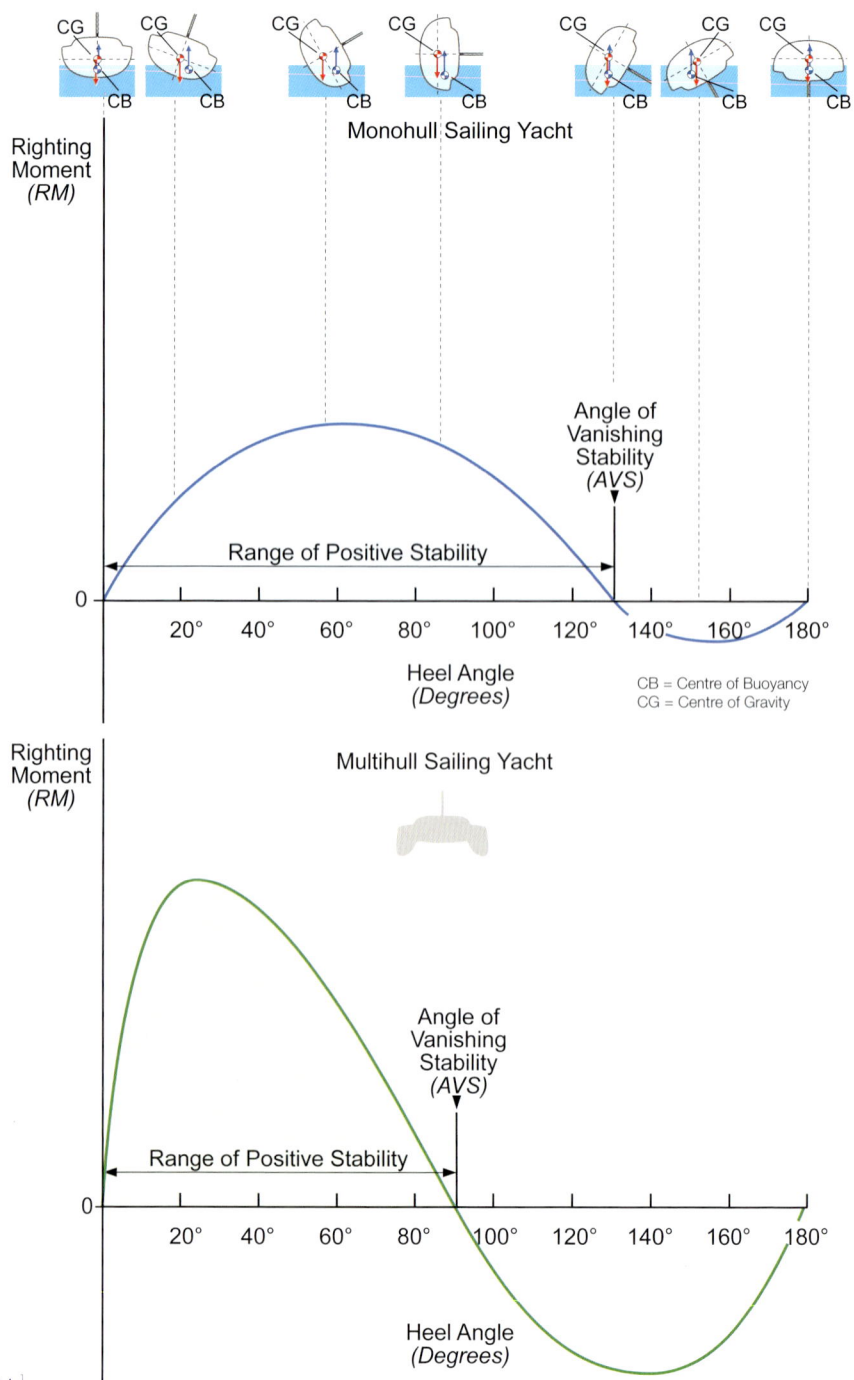

**Monohull Sailing Yacht**

Righting Moment (RM) vs Heel Angle (Degrees)

- Range of Positive Stability
- Angle of Vanishing Stability (AVS)

CB = Centre of Buoyancy
CG = Centre of Gravity

**Multihull Sailing Yacht**

Righting Moment (RM) vs Heel Angle (Degrees)

- Range of Positive Stability
- Angle of Vanishing Stability (AVS)

[14]

Stability

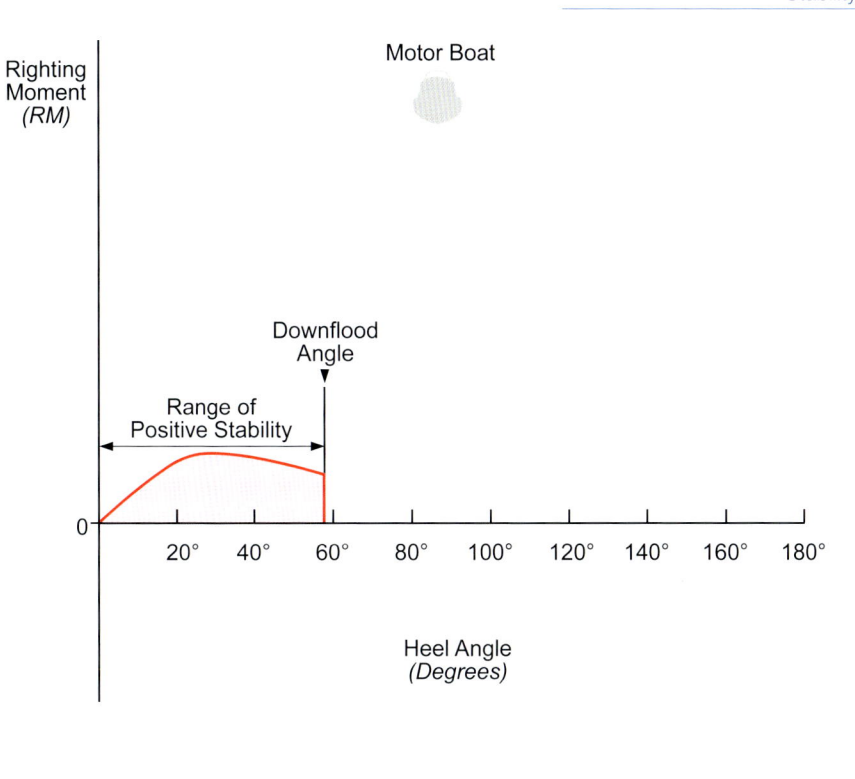

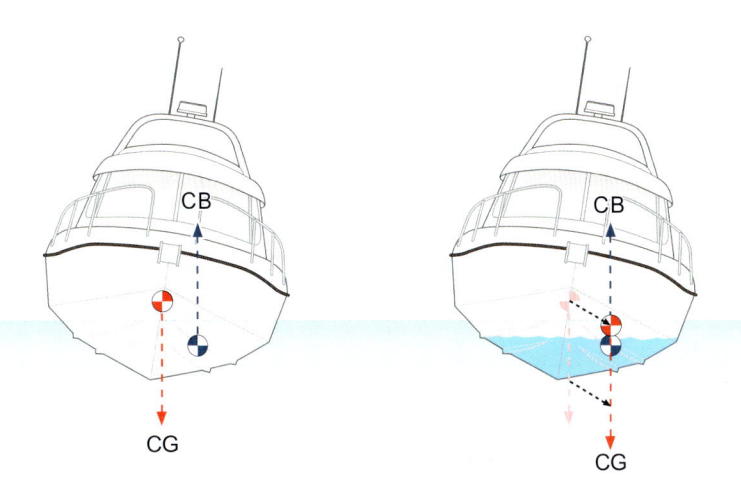

## Motor Boat

Righting Moment (RM)

Range of Positive Stability

Downflood Angle

0 — 20° 40° 60° 80° 100° 120° 140° 160° 180°

Heel Angle (Degrees)

CB — CG

CB — CG

Free-surface effect allows the mass of water in a boat to move its centre of gravity. In this example, the AVS is reduced to 15° by the mass of water in the bilges.

# Types of Sailing Yacht

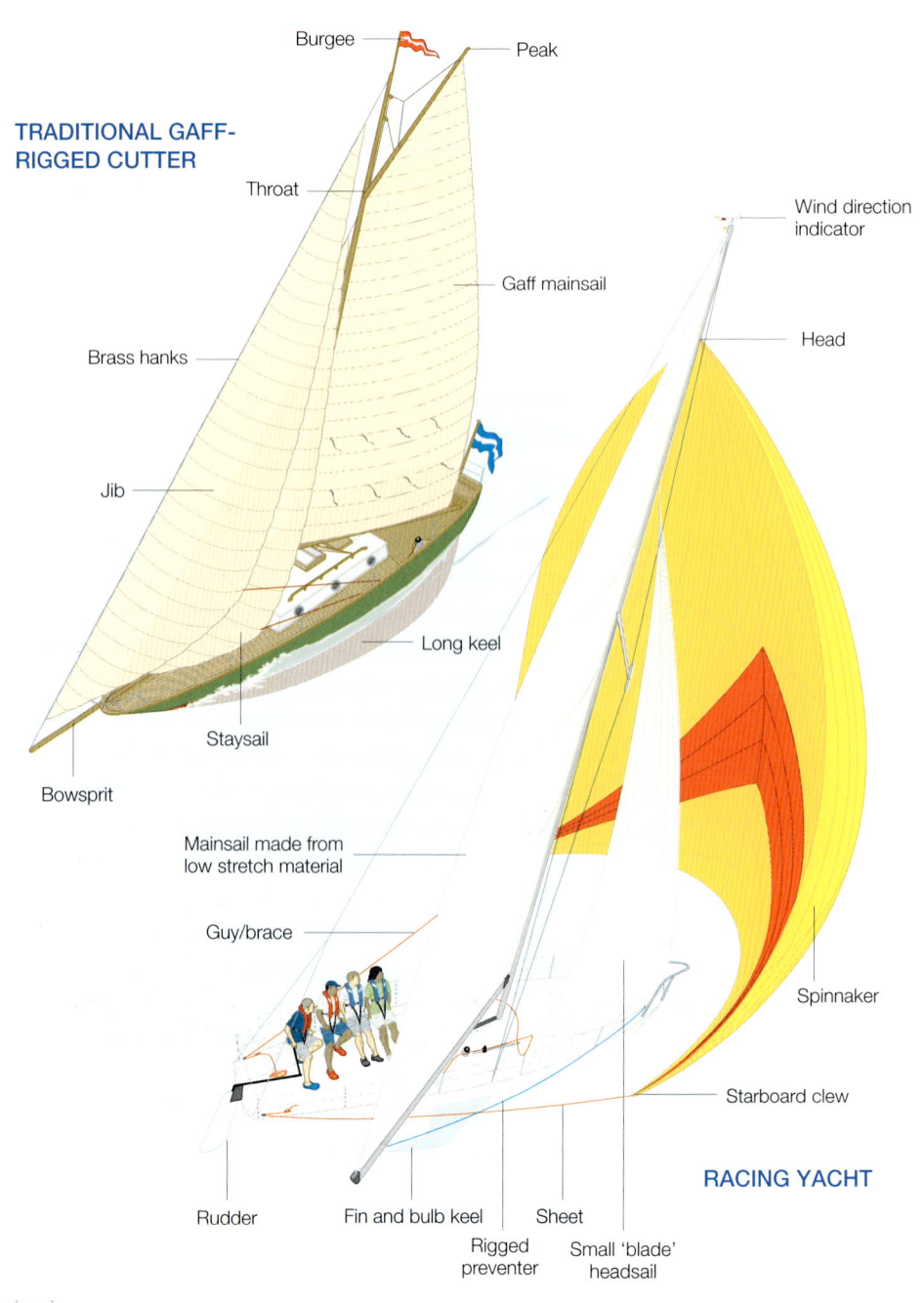

**TRADITIONAL GAFF-RIGGED CUTTER**

- Burgee
- Peak
- Throat
- Gaff mainsail
- Brass hanks
- Jib
- Long keel
- Staysail
- Bowsprit

**RACING YACHT**

- Wind direction indicator
- Head
- Mainsail made from low stretch material
- Guy/brace
- Spinnaker
- Starboard clew
- Rudder
- Fin and bulb keel
- Sheet
- Rigged preventer
- Small 'blade' headsail

Types of Sailing Yacht

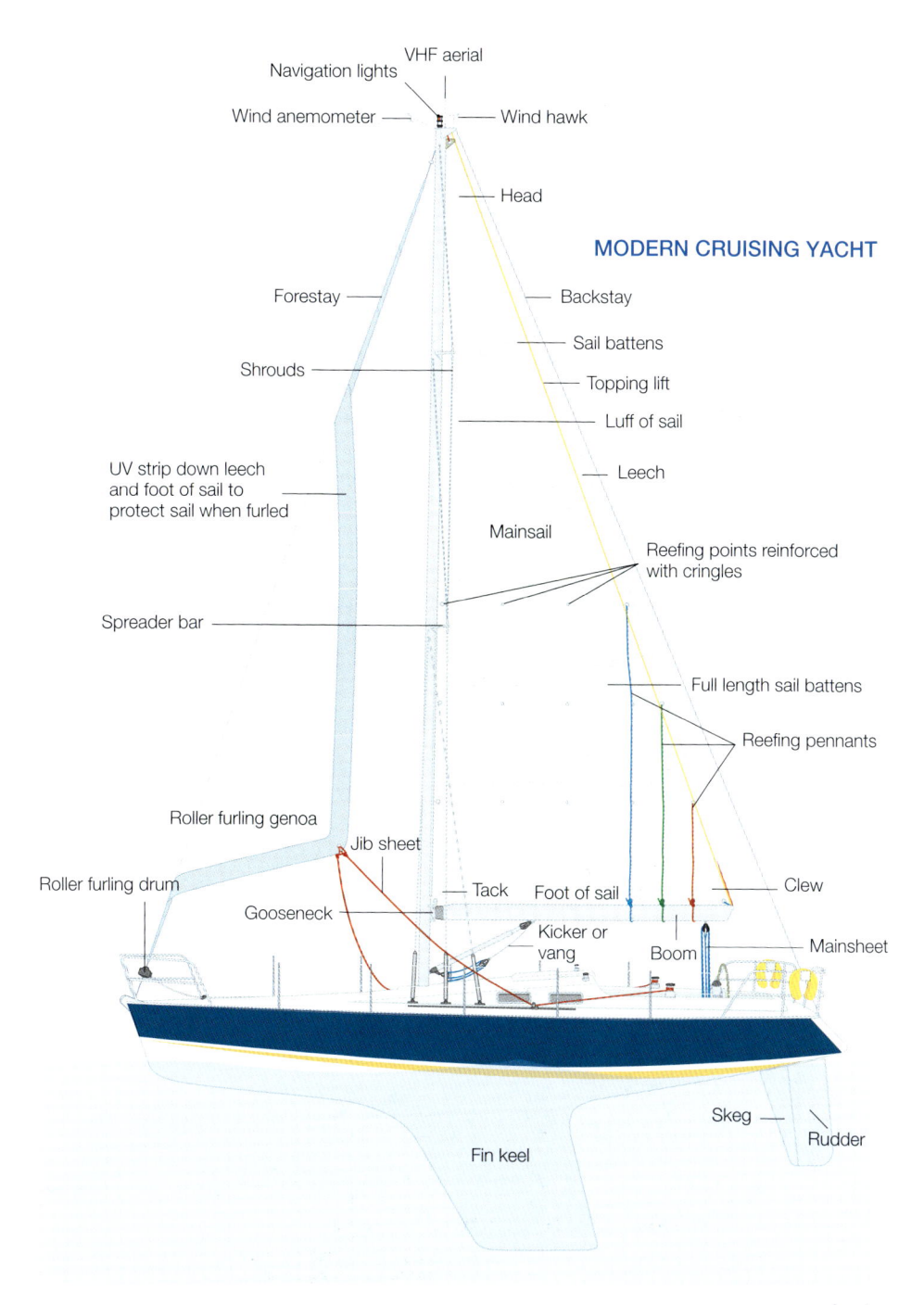

## MODERN CRUISING YACHT

# Types of Motor Vessel

### Flybridge Motor Cruiser

High-performance planing craft powered by twin inboard engines or twin outdrives. Many are capable of speeds exceeding 30 knots in smooth or moderate conditions.

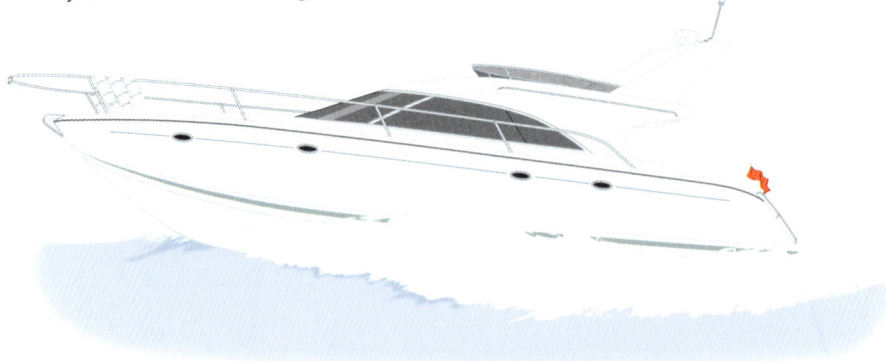

Widely used in leisure cruising and can also be commonly chartered.

### Semi-displacement Craft

Hull partially rises onto the plane. Fine entry means a comfortable ride when going into a head sea.

## RIB (Rigid Inflatable Boat)

Fast open boat – separate inflatable compartments make it almost unsinkable.

## Displacement Craft

Travels through rather than over the water. This conventional hull type is slower than planing craft but has good sea-keeping properties.

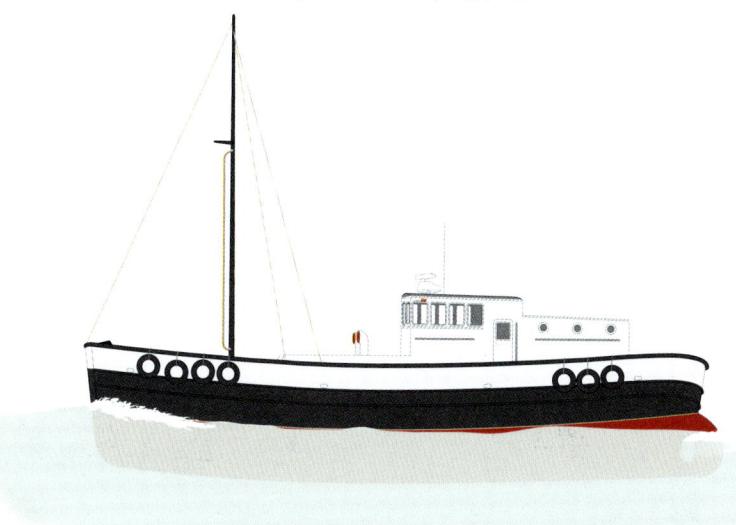

*Types of Motor Vessel*

## High-Performance Planing Craft

The boat rides over the surface of the water.

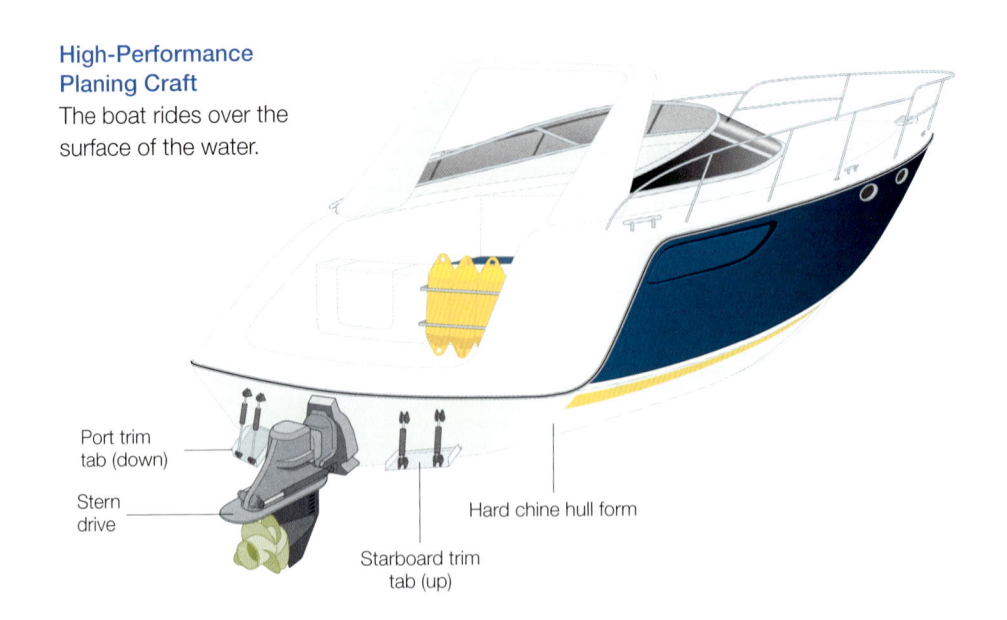

Port trim tab (down)

Stern drive

Hard chine hull form

Starboard trim tab (up)

## Stern Drive

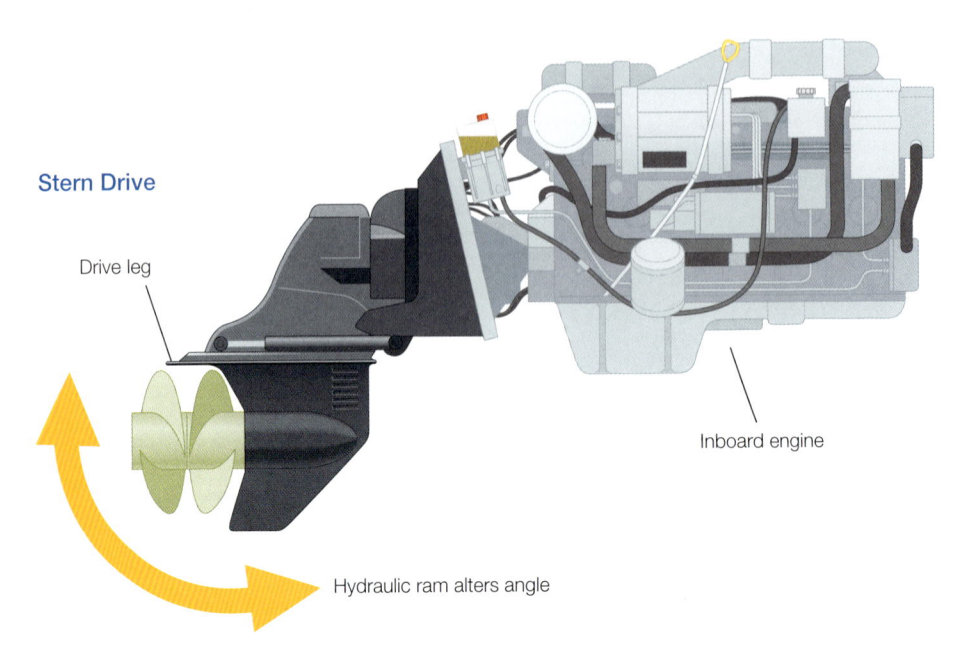

Drive leg

Inboard engine

Hydraulic ram alters angle

[ 20 ]

## TRIM

Changing the trim will affect the way a boat behaves in different conditions. Experiment to find out how your boat reacts.

Power trim (head sea)

Outdrive leg in – drops the bow for going into a head sea and reduces slamming.

Power trim (following sea)

Outdrive leg out – lifts the bow in a following sea.

Types of Motor Vessel

## Trim Tabs in Operation

**Trim tabs (head sea)**

Both tabs down = Bow down.

**Trim tabs (following sea)**

Both tabs up = Bow up.

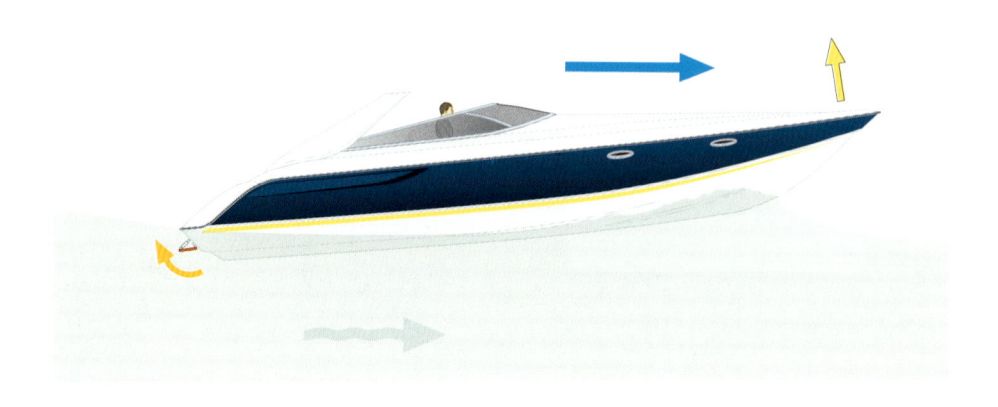

Types of Motor Vessel

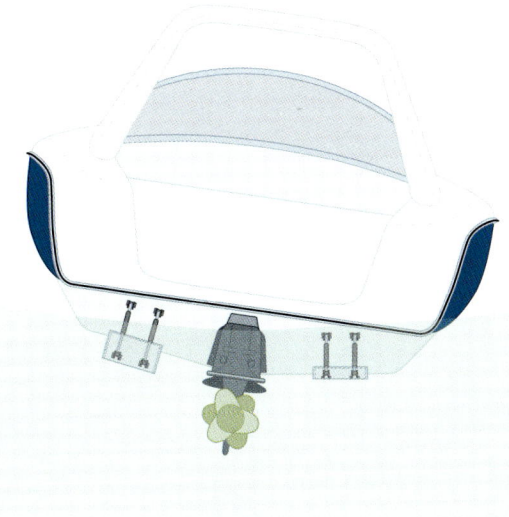

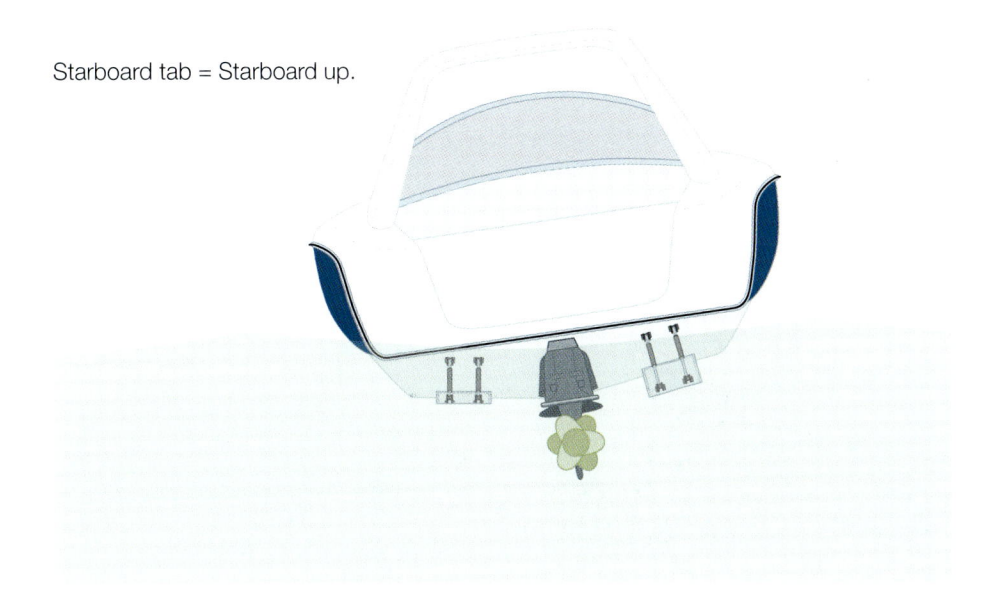

Port tab = Port up.

Starboard tab = Starboard up.

# Knots

Just a few knots will get you sailing. They are easy to tie with a bit of practice and you will find them very useful.

## Figure-of-eight
Used as a stopper knot to prevent a rope running through a car or jammer.

## Clove hitch
For tying on fenders or other uses such as lashing the tiller amidships.

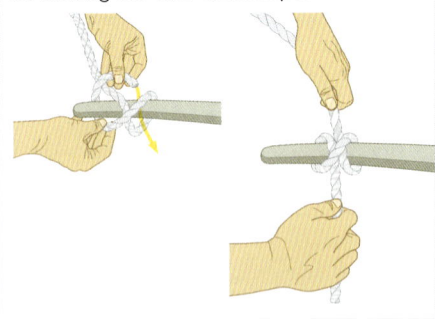

## Rolling hitch
Used for temporarily relieving the strain on a working rope, e.g. if you have a riding turn (jam) on a winch.

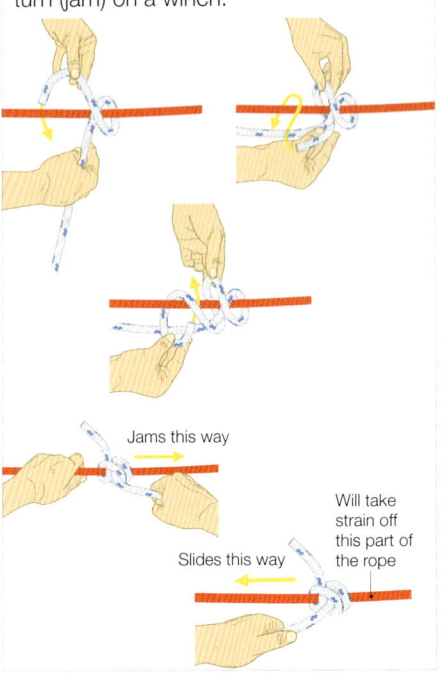

Jams this way

Slides this way

Will take strain off this part of the rope

## Bowline
Makes a loop in the end of a rope. Used to attach the jib sheets or to make a loop for mooring.

Knots

### Round turn and two half-hitches
A versatile knot with many uses, such as securing a mooring line to a ring or hanging a fender.

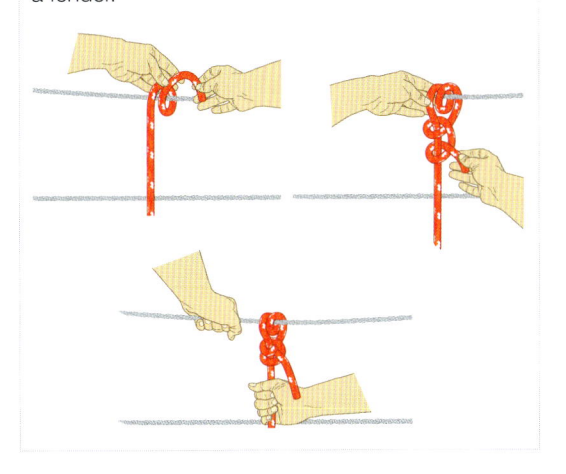

### Reef knot
Useful to tie in reefs to tidy the sail – but not secure enough for mooring lines.

### Single sheet bend
Used to join two ropes – useful to lengthen a mooring line.

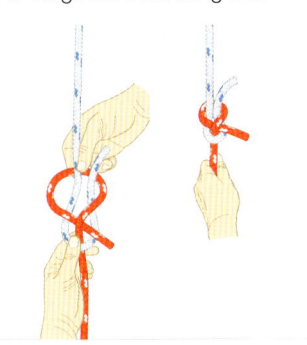

### Double sheet bend
More secure and is also used to tie a smaller line to a larger one.

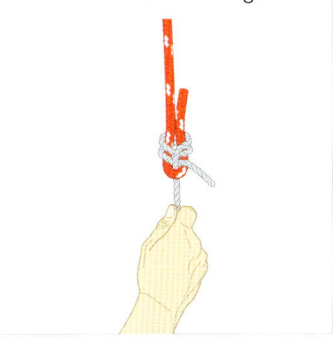

[ 25 ]

# Ropework

## Making Fast to a Cleat

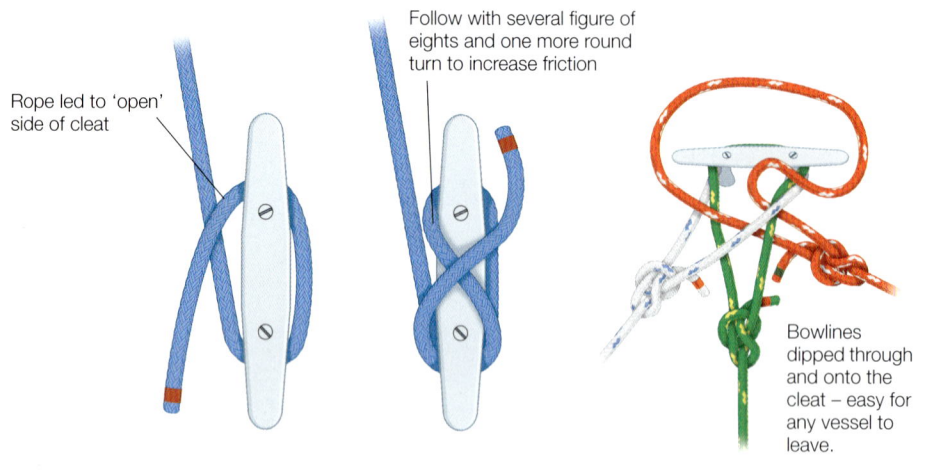

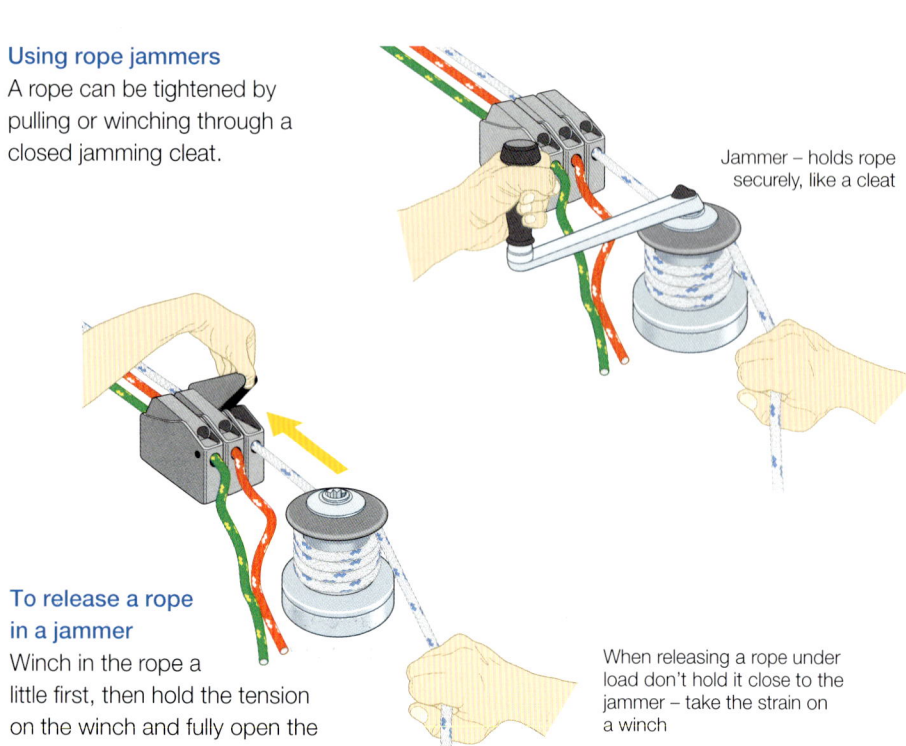

Rope led to 'open' side of cleat

Follow with several figure of eights and one more round turn to increase friction

Bowlines dipped through and onto the cleat – easy for any vessel to leave.

## Using rope jammers

A rope can be tightened by pulling or winching through a closed jamming cleat.

Jammer – holds rope securely, like a cleat

## To release a rope in a jammer

Winch in the rope a little first, then hold the tension on the winch and fully open the jammer.

When releasing a rope under load don't hold it close to the jammer – take the strain on a winch

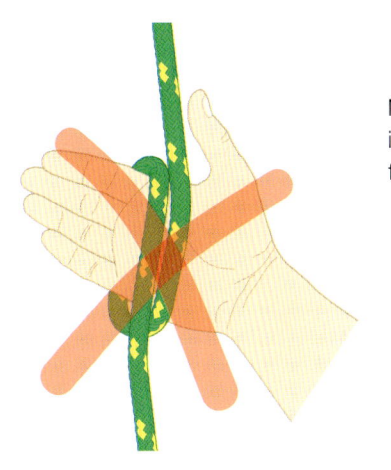

Ropework

Never wrap rope round your hand when holding it, pulling on it, or using a winch. Keep hands and fingers away from winches and jammers.

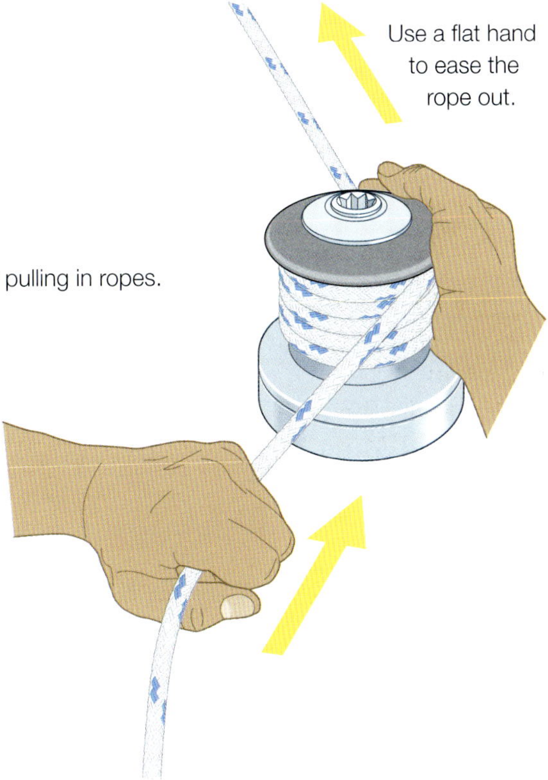

Use a flat hand to ease the rope out.

**Winching Techniques**
Using a winch gives more power for pulling in ropes.

Always have your thumbs uppermost. Take care not to trap fingers or thumbs between the rope and the winch.

Never wrap the rope around your hand.

# Mooring Alongside

## ALONGSIDE A WALL
Use a separate line for each task.

When you have attached a warp to a bollard/ring etc., bring the rest of the line back on board and attach it to a cleat. Each warp can then be independently adjusted from on board as the tide rises and falls.

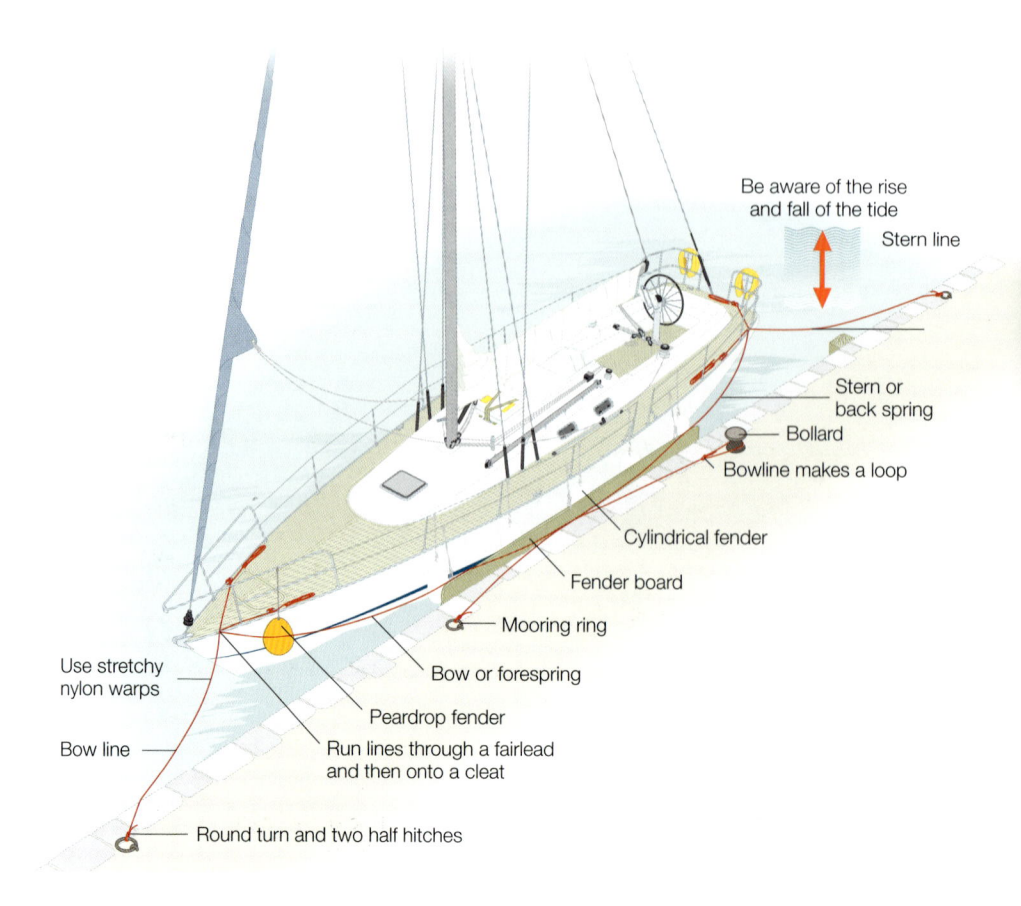

Be aware of the rise and fall of the tide

Stern line

Stern or back spring

Bollard

Bowline makes a loop

Cylindrical fender

Fender board

Mooring ring

Bow or forespring

Use stretchy nylon warps

Peardrop fender

Bow line

Run lines through a fairlead and then onto a cleat

Round turn and two half hitches

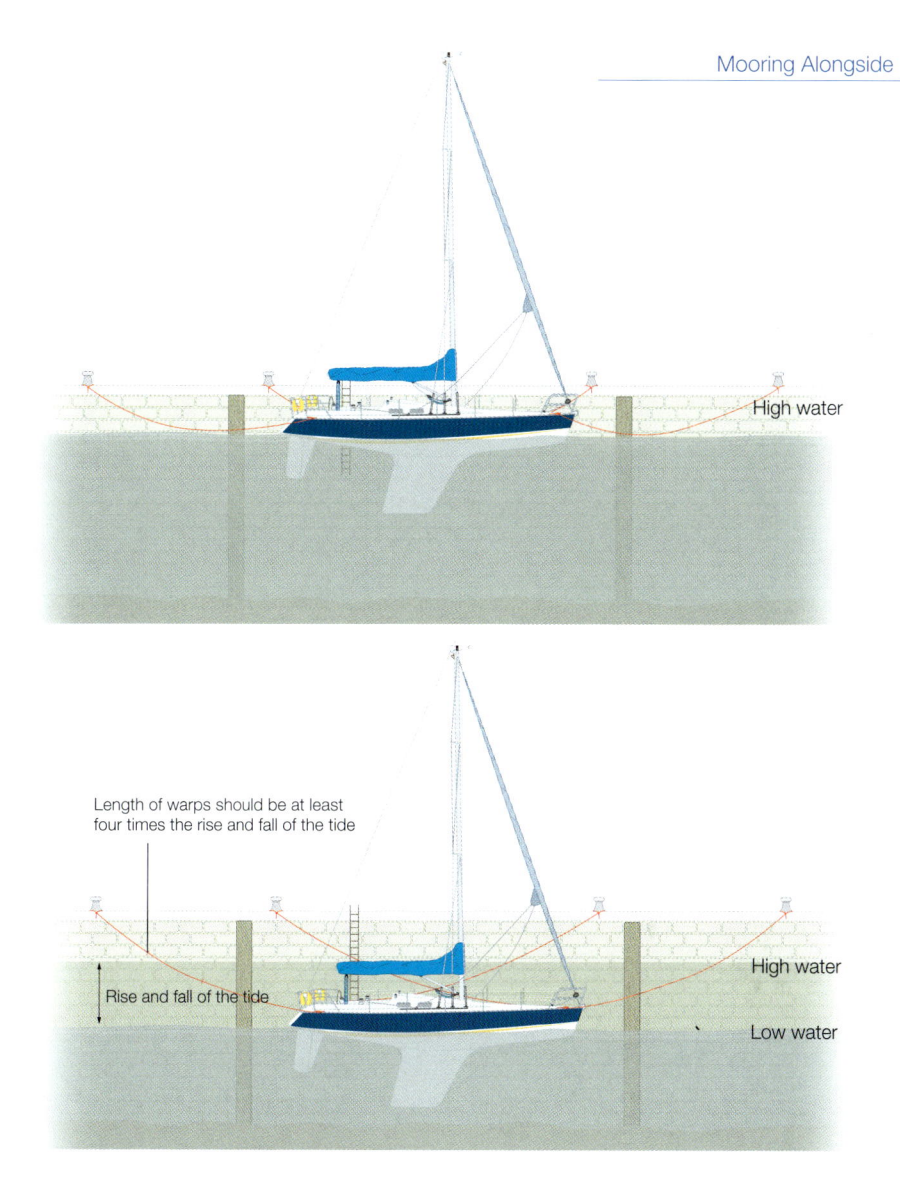

Mooring Alongside

Length of warps should be at least four times the rise and fall of the tide

Rise and fall of the tide

High water

Low water

The length of the warps should be at least four times the rise and fall of tide.

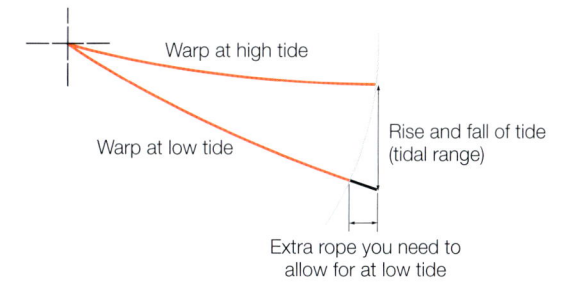

Warp at high tide

Warp at low tide

Rise and fall of tide (tidal range)

Extra rope you need to allow for at low tide

## Mooring Alongside

### In a Raft

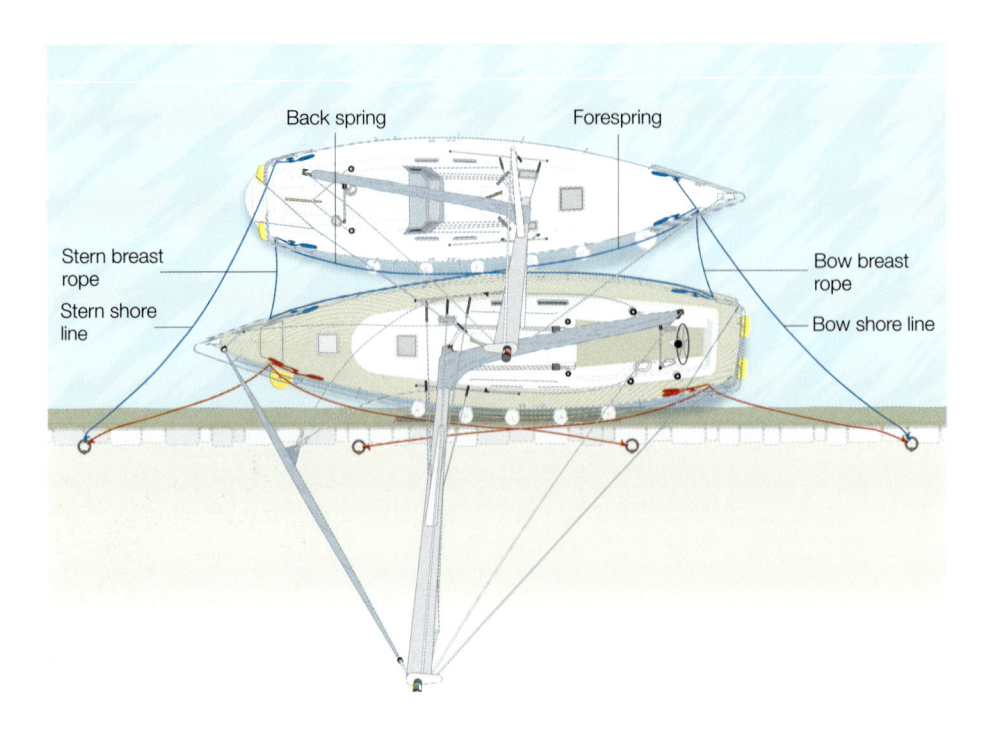

Back spring | Forespring

Stern breast rope
Stern shore line

Bow breast rope
Bow shore line

The outside boat should always take bow and stern lines ashore to minimise strain on the other boat's shore lines and cleats.

Any subsequent boats should also run shore, breast and spring lines to the adjacent boat and the mooring. A good skipper does not rely on the other boats' fittings or the competence of the other crew.

In a raft it would be best for the second boat to be in the opposite direction to the first. This will ensure that both boats have a bit of privacy from each other as the cockpits will be further apart. It will also be easier to use the foredeck of the other boat to get ashore. The masts should be staggered so the rigging will not get tangled when the boats roll.

Mooring Alongside

## ON A FLOATING PONTOON

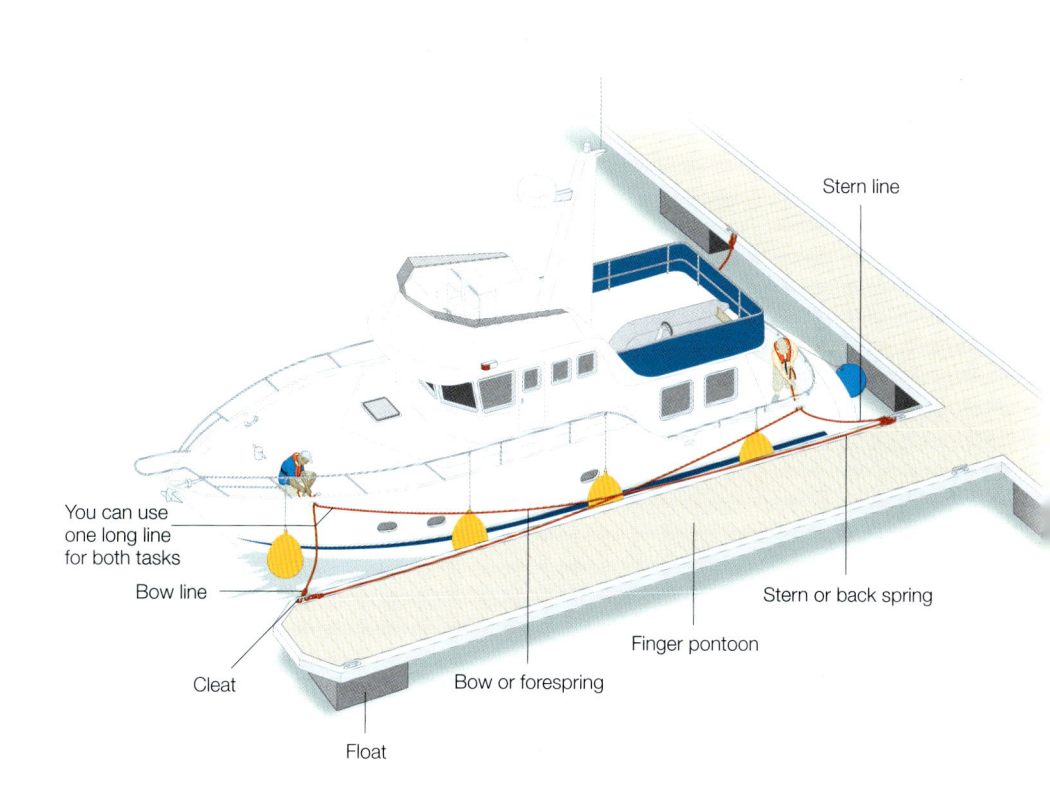

Stern line

You can use one long line for both tasks

Bow line

Cleat

Bow or forespring

Finger pontoon

Stern or back spring

Float

You should not have to adjust lines as the tide rises and falls.

[ 31 ]

Mooring Alongside

## IN A PEN

Stern lines are attached to piles and the bow lines are attached to a wall or pontoon. Usually the windward lines are attached first.

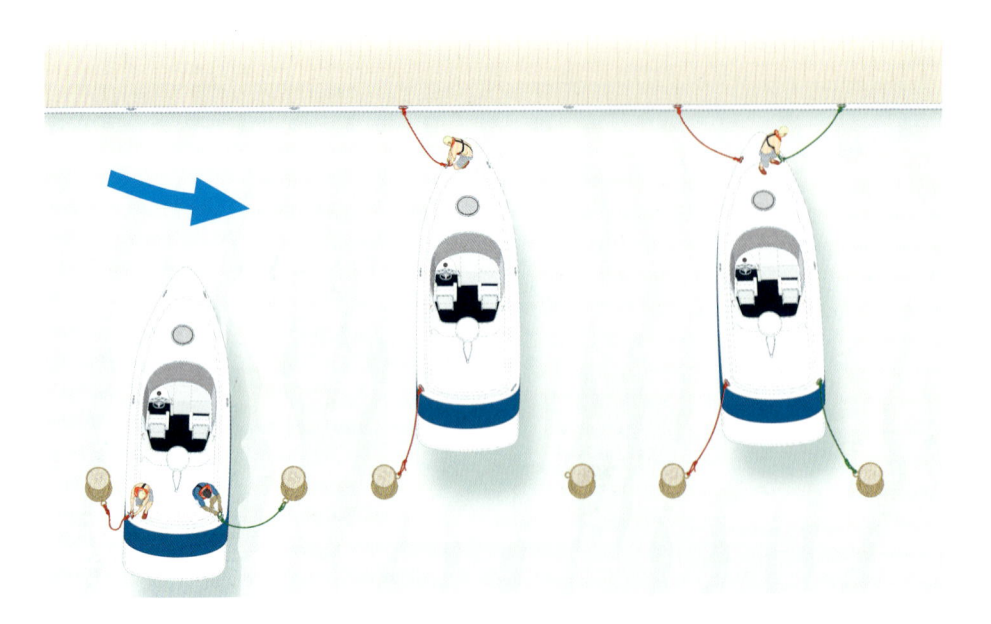

In some countries one of the piles is replaced by a pontoon for ease of access to the shore. The lines are adjusted to allow access from the steps or amidships. Pick-up lines are usually supplied on the piles to aid retrieval.

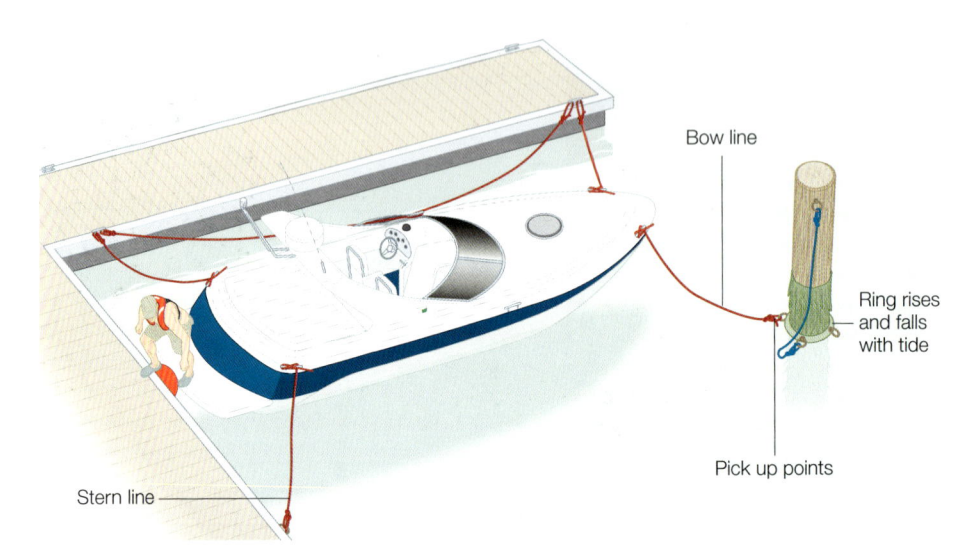

Bow line

Ring rises and falls with tide

Pick up points

Stern line

# Anchoring

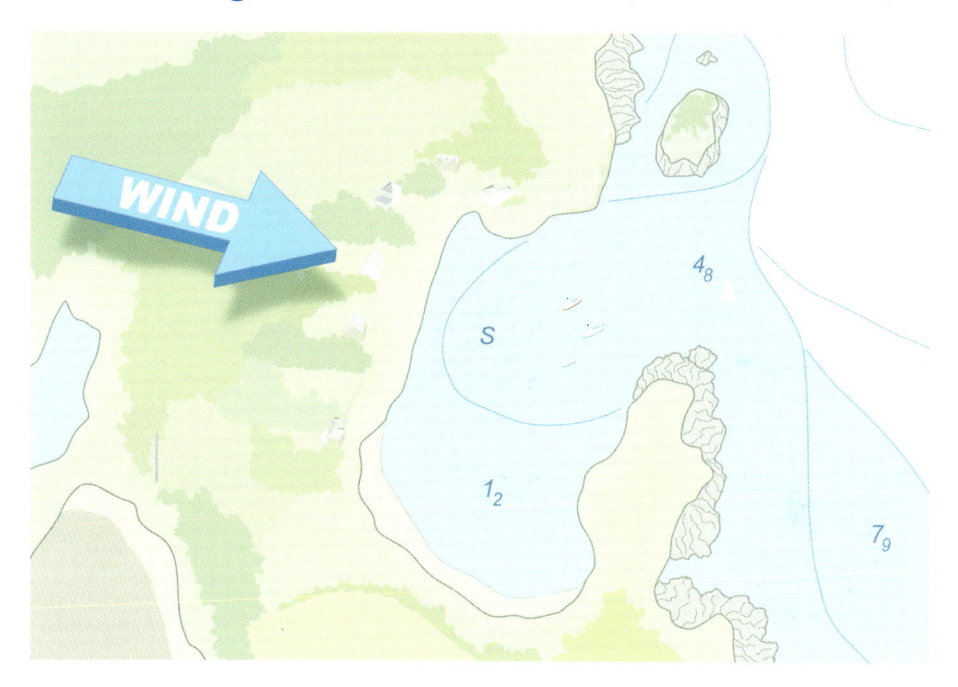

Will you be sheltered? Look for maximum protection from wind, swell and tide. Check forecast for possible changes of wind direction.

What is the sea bed like? Look at the chart symbols – mud and sand give better holding than rock or shingle.

What will the tide do during your stay? Calculate the times and heights. Make sure that you don't pick a spot where you will go aground as the tide falls.

Will you have enough swinging room? Allow for other boats, isolated rocks, etc.

Prepare the amount of anchor chain or warp that you need before dropping the anchor.

You don't necessarily need to anchor at the position of the anchor symbol. This is just a recommendation.

Avoid anchoring on or near the leading line – other boats may be coming in.

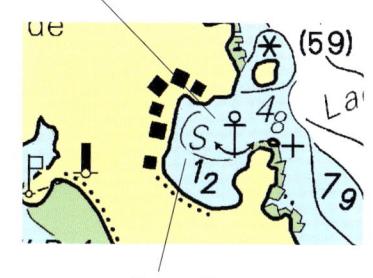

There will be much less tidal flow in the bay than outside.

Anchoring

## TYPES OF ANCHOR

**Delta**
Good holding-to-weight ratio. Designed to stay on bow roller for self-launching.

**Bruce**
Good holding-to-weight ratio. Awkward to store in a small anchor locker.

**Danforth**
Good holding-to-weight ratio. Stows flat. Can be hard to break out of mud.

Anchoring

### CQR or Plough
Good holding-to-weight ratio. Hard to stow and moving parts can capsize.

### Fisherman's
Traditional type. Good for rocky and weedy bottoms. Awkward to stow and poor holding power in sand and mud.

### Grapnel
Normally quite light. Awkward to stow unless it's a collapsing model. Good in coral or rock. Poor in mud, clay or sand. Better suited to a tender than as a vessel's main anchor.

Anchoring

## Anchoring Terminology

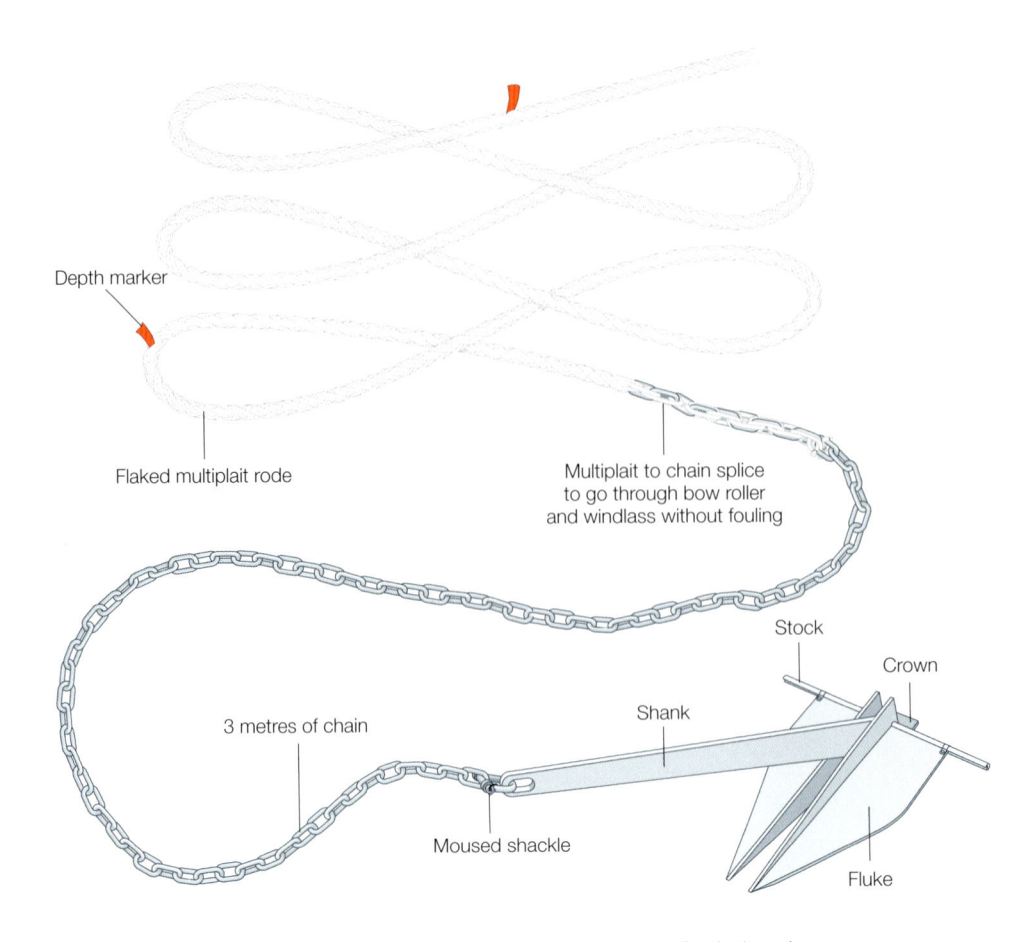

Depth marker

Flaked multiplait rode

Multiplait to chain splice
to go through bow roller
and windlass without fouling

3 metres of chain

Moused shackle

Stock

Crown

Shank

Fluke

Danforth anchor

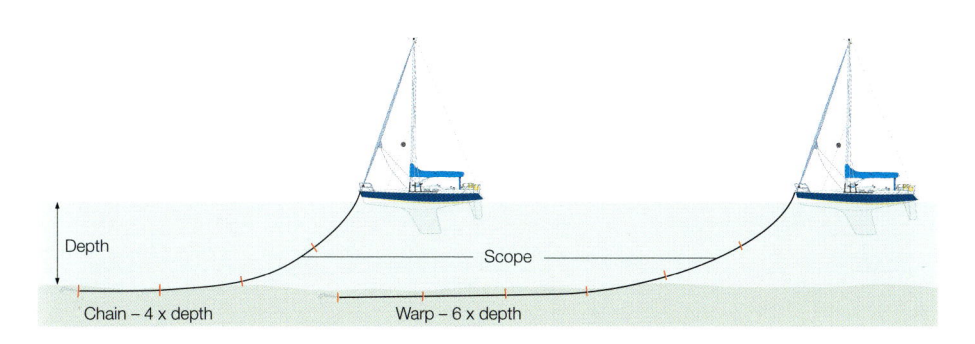

Anchoring

Depth | Scope
Chain – 4 x depth | Warp – 6 x depth

## Scope
The scope of chain or warp you need depends on the maximum depth of water you expect during your stay.

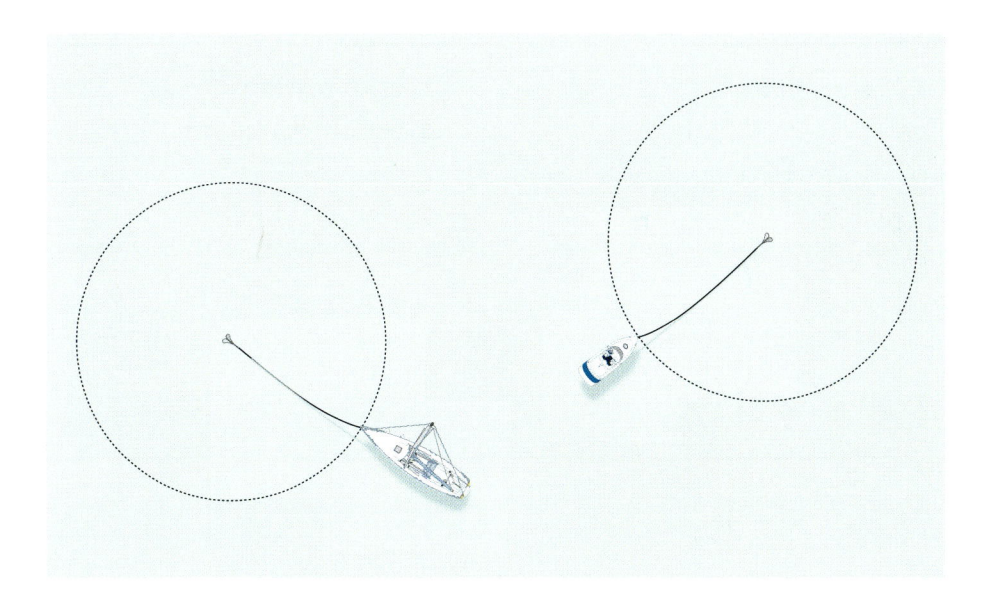

Always allow enough swinging room to account for wind and tide. Bear in mind that light/flat-bottomed boats will lie differently to deeper draught/low windage boats.

Safety Equipment

# Safety Equipment

As skipper you are responsible for the safety of your crew, the condition of your vessel and all equipment on board!

It is advisable to take training courses in first aid, navigation and how to fire flares. You should also have a basic knowledge of how to make running repairs to your vessel while at sea.

Working navigation lights conforming to correct specifications

Fire blanket in the galley – do not stow directly above the cooker

Soft wood bungs for plugging broken skin fittings and holes, and a wooden mallet. These should always be kept together

Extra warps can be very useful

Bucket with sponge, bailer and hand bilge pump (useful for confined spaces)

High-visibility sheet with the boat's name, for identification from the air

Spare water and fuel with funnel

Red hand flares, red parachute flares, orange pinpoint flares and orange buoyant smoke.
All should be contained within a waterproof polybottle with the lid on at all times.
This will keep flares dry and protect them from accidental ignition

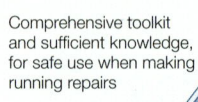

Comprehensive toolkit and sufficient knowledge, for safe use when making running repairs

Powerful searchlight

Various engine spares – impeller, fuel filters, belts etc

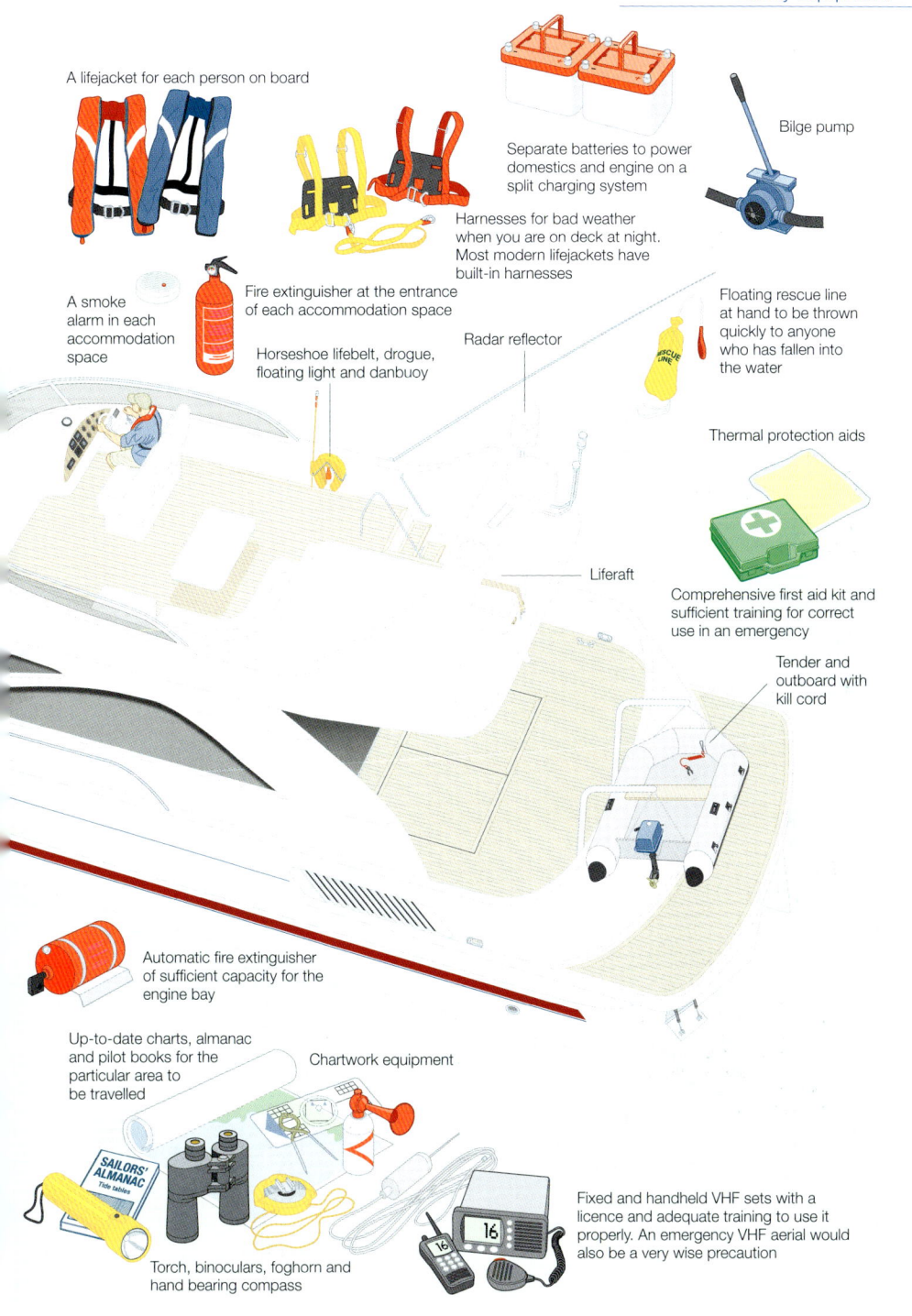

## Safety Equipment

A lifejacket for each person on board

Separate batteries to power domestics and engine on a split charging system

Bilge pump

Harnesses for bad weather when you are on deck at night. Most modern lifejackets have built-in harnesses

A smoke alarm in each accommodation space

Fire extinguisher at the entrance of each accommodation space

Floating rescue line at hand to be thrown quickly to anyone who has fallen into the water

Horseshoe lifebelt, drogue, floating light and danbuoy

Radar reflector

Thermal protection aids

Liferaft

Comprehensive first aid kit and sufficient training for correct use in an emergency

Tender and outboard with kill cord

Automatic fire extinguisher of sufficient capacity for the engine bay

Up-to-date charts, almanac and pilot books for the particular area to be travelled

Chartwork equipment

Torch, binoculars, foghorn and hand bearing compass

Fixed and handheld VHF sets with a licence and adequate training to use it properly. An emergency VHF aerial would also be a very wise precaution

Personal Safety and Comfort

# Personal Safety and Comfort

## Clothing
Man-made fibres layered to trap air for warmth. Avoid wearing cotton clothing underneath waterproofs.

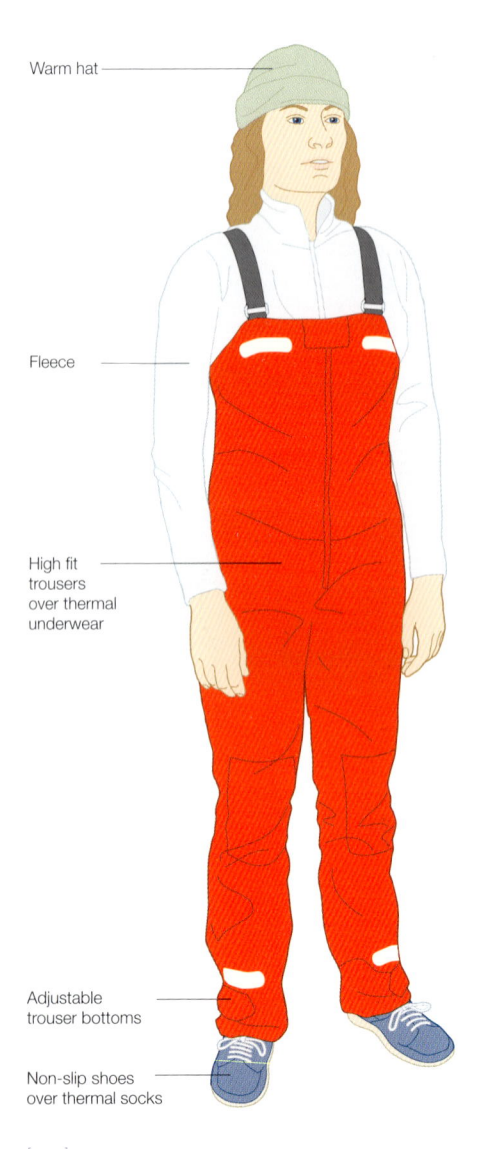

## Seasickness & Hypothermia

Stay warm and dry.

Eat and drink regularly.

Take or use seasickness remedies.

Warm hat

Fleece

High fit trousers over thermal underwear

Adjustable trouser bottoms

Non-slip shoes over thermal socks

Personal Safety and Comfort

### Symptoms of Seasickness
Lethargic/disinterested. Pale colour.

### Symptoms of Hypothermia
Shivering, pale colour, irrational behaviour, disorientated.

### Sun Protection
Ultraviolet rays are harmful, may cause skin cancer and impair vision.

Reflection from the water increases the effect of the sun.

Wear a wide-brimmed hat and/or one with neck protection. Use sunglasses with 100 per cent UV protection.

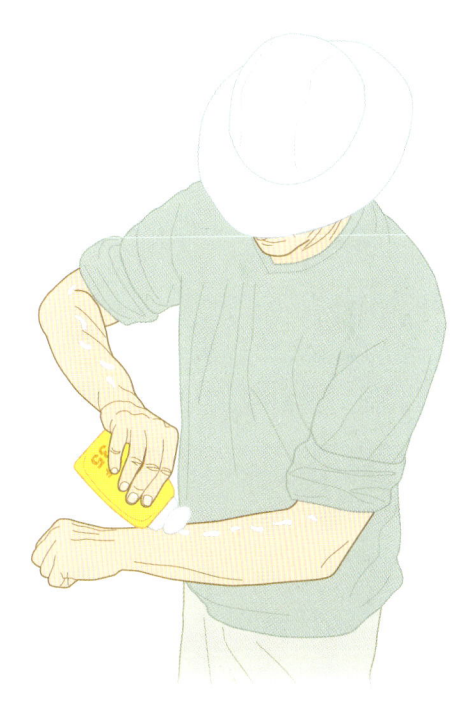

Regularly apply sunblock of SPF 30–40.

Personal Safety and Comfort

Wear loose, long-sleeved shirts and trousers.

Try to avoid exposure between 11 a.m. and 3 p.m. Take a long lunch and seek shade. Biminis and cockpit tents are ideal shelters.

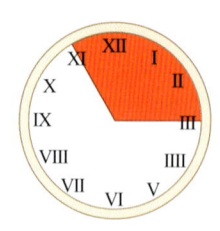

Babies and toddlers are especially susceptible to UV damage. Keep them out of the sun or well protected.

Wear shoes to protect feet from hot decks and stubbing toes.

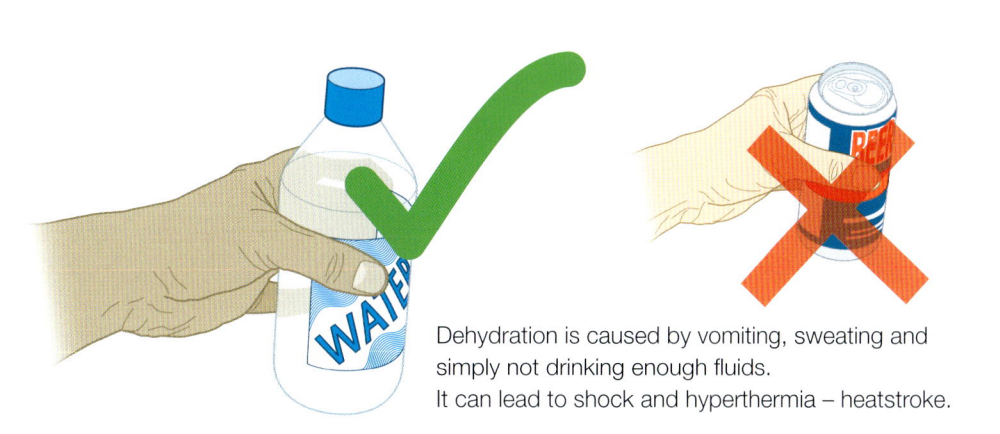

Dehydration is caused by vomiting, sweating and simply not drinking enough fluids.
It can lead to shock and hyperthermia – heatstroke.

## Dehydration Symptoms

Mild: Thirst, dry lips, dark urine colour. Remedy: Rehydrate using water and/or with an oral rehydrating solution.

Moderate: Partial heatstroke. Very dry mouth, sunken eyes, skin loses elasticity. Remedy: Rehydrate casualty under close supervision and seek medical guidance.

Severe: Heatstroke. All of above plus rapid, weak pulse, rapid breathing, confusion, lethargy. Remedy: Get medical help quickly and rehydrate.

DON'T EXCEED THE ALCOHOL LIMIT.

# Fire Safety

## Common Causes of Fire

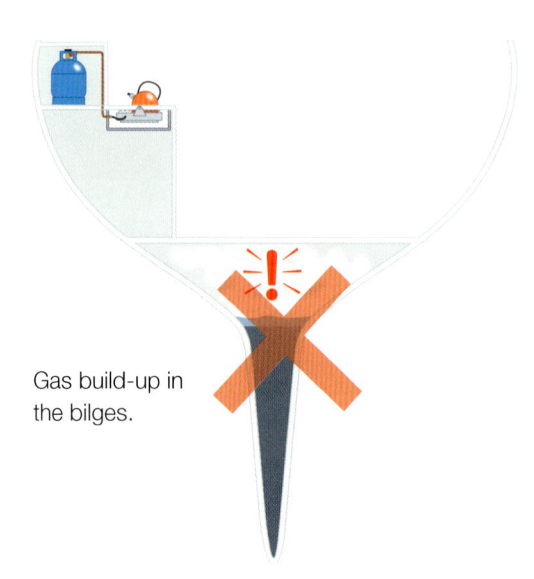

Smoking below decks.

Solvents/paints stored below.

Faulty wiring.

Gas build-up in the bilges.

Cooking fats.

Fire Safety

## Extinguishers
Dry powder – don't use on flammable liquids.
$CO_2$/Halocarbon – good for enclosed spaces.
AFFF – foam. Good for flammable liquids.
Blanket – good for smothering flames and if clothing is on fire.

## Petrol/Gasoline Vapour
Always vent engine space before starting an inboard petrol engine.

Keep outboards on deck to avoid the build-up of petrol vapour below.

## Gas Safety
Butane and propane can be highly dangerous.

To clear gas, open hatches and turn downwind to vent fresh air through the boat.

Bilge pumps are designed to pump water. Many won't clear gas very effectively. Use of electric bilge pumps should be avoided if a gas leak is suspected.

Don't attempt DIY repairs to your system. Always call in a qualified fitter.

Keep gas bottle in a sealed locker that drains overboard

Drainage hole

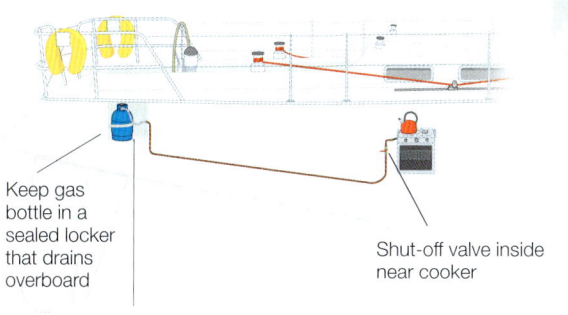

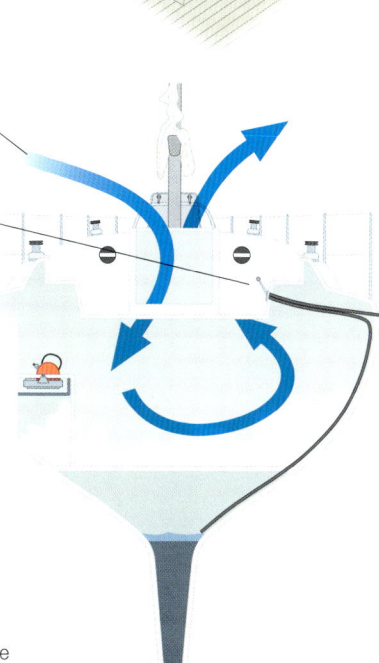

Shut-off valve inside near cooker

[ 45 ]

Fire Fighting

# Fire Fighting

### Location of Extinguishers
Extinguishers should be to hand near the exit to each accommodation space.

The engine space should have its own dedicated extinguisher which is automatic or can be activated remotely without having to open the engine compartment and let in oxygen.

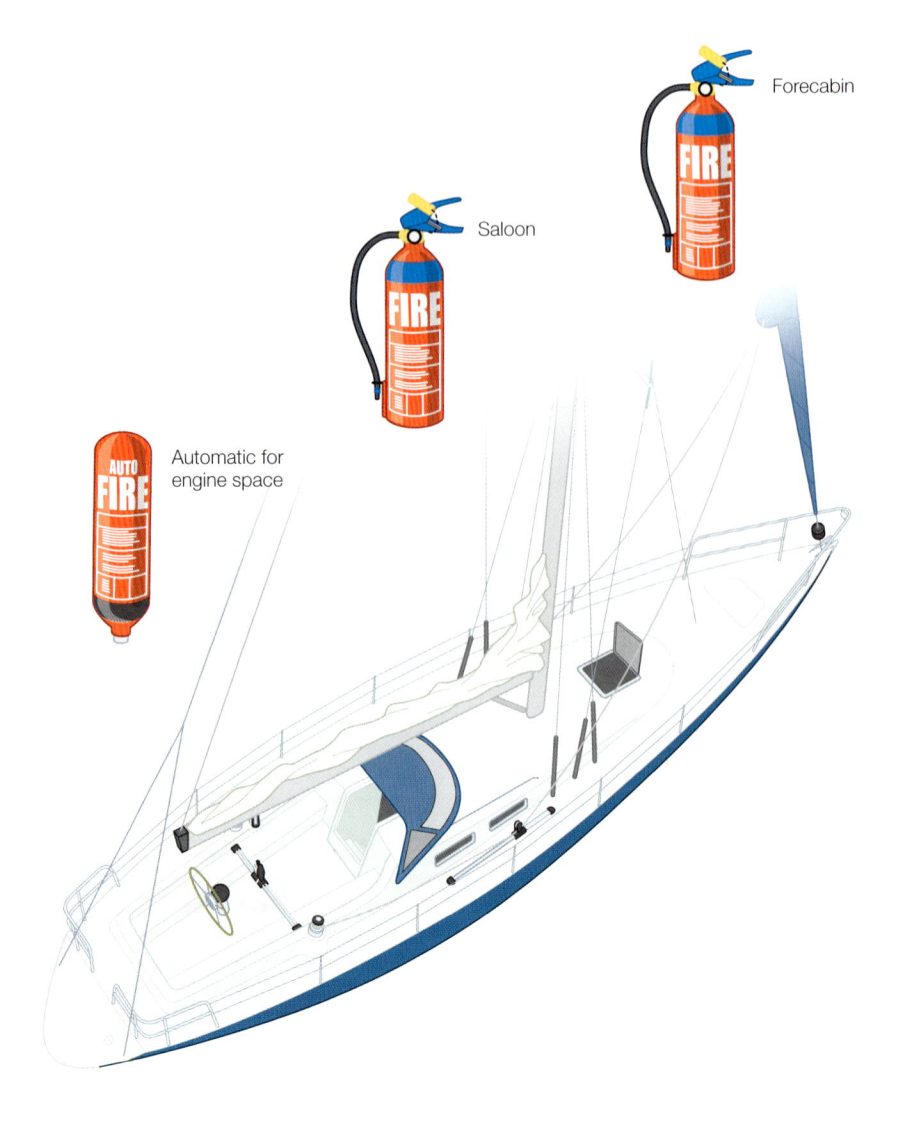

Forecabin

Saloon

Automatic for engine space

Fire Fighting

## Fighting the Fire

Aim the extinguisher at the base of the flames.

Splashing water from a bucket can be more effective than throwing its entire contents at once.

Fire blankets can be used to smother a galley fire. Protect your hands when using a fire blanket.

They are also essential for clothing fires.

If you cannot fight the fire, be prepared to abandon ship.

Remember: The boat will fill up with smoke very quickly. Get everyone on deck with a lifejacket. You may have to send a Mayday/fire distress flares etc.

[ 47 ]

Emergency Procedures

# Emergency Procedures

Boating is generally a safe pastime but, should the worst happen, make sure you and your crew know what to do.

If you are not already wearing one, put on a lifejacket.

Alert the coastguard.

Use a pinpoint flare (night) or an orange smoke (day).

## ABANDONING TO THE LIFERAFT

Throw to leeward and tug painter to inflate. Make sure the painter is tied on.

Board raft from the yacht. Stay dry. Put heaviest, strongest crew in first to stabilise the raft and assist others in boarding.

Once aboard:
- Cut painter
- Paddle away
- Stream drogue
- Close door
- Take seasickness tablets
- Keep as warm and dry as possible
- Ventilate interior every hour

# Cold Shock

1 You will most likely gasp for air, then breathe rapidly. You can only hold your breath for a few seconds – protect your airway from waves and spray.

2 Your heart will be working harder, so don't try to swim – just relax!

3 The effects will be at their worst in the first 30 seconds but will have gone within three minutes.

4 Being prepared for this to happen so that you don't panic will greatly reduce the risk.

Emergency Services

# Emergency Services

### RESCUE
The lifeboat coxswain will need to talk to you to assess the situation.

Make sure there are no lines in the water which could foul the lifeboat's propeller.

Any casualties will be taken off.

You may be taken in tow but the lifeboat's priority is to save lives, not salvage boats. Attach tow line to strong points via a bridle.

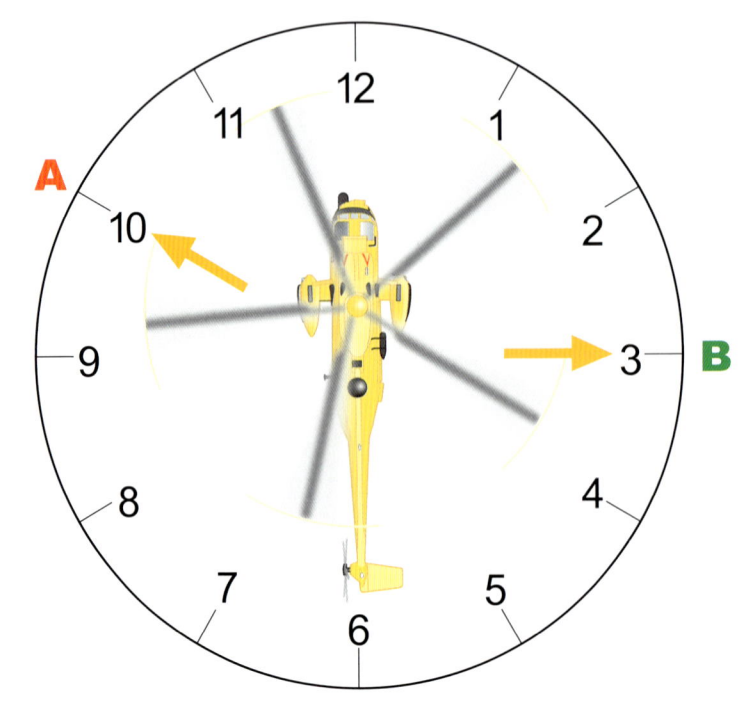

You will probably see or hear the helicopter before they see you. Call them on *VHF Channel 16* and give them your position and distance, *in relation to the helicopter*, using the clock notation above (for example, if you were 'A', "I am at your 10'clock" or 'B' "I am at your 3 o'clock"), even if you have triggered an EPIRB for them to home in on. Use a pinpoint flare (at night) or orange smoke (daytime) for them to locate your position from a distance once they know which direction to look.

Emergency Services

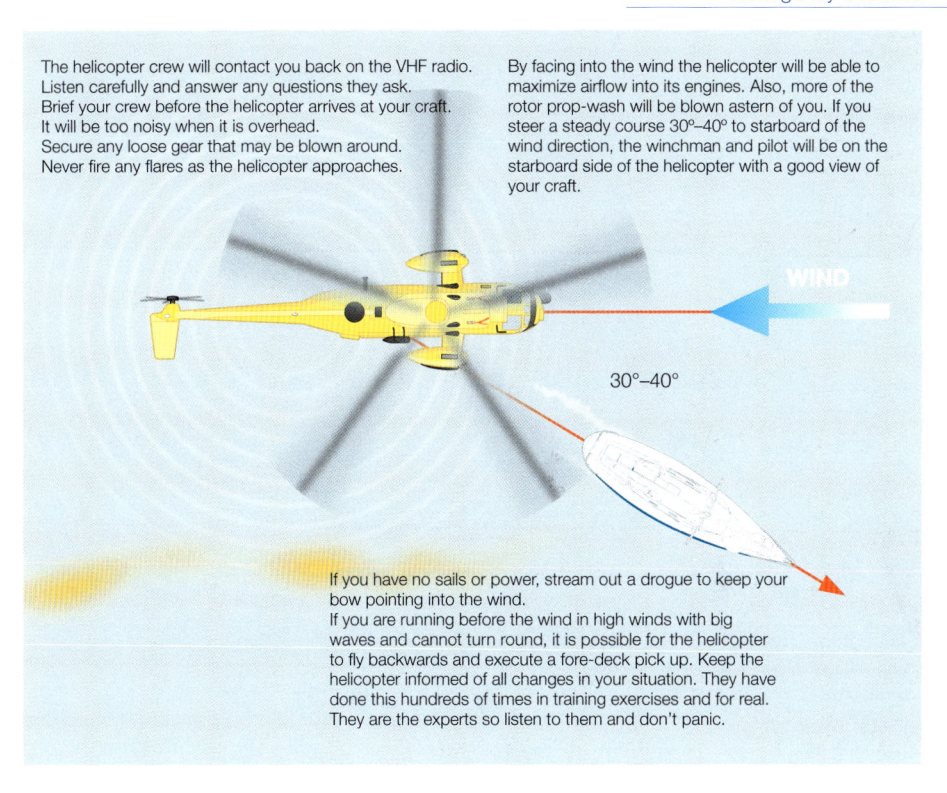

The helicopter crew will contact you back on the VHF radio. Listen carefully and answer any questions they ask. Brief your crew before the helicopter arrives at your craft. It will be too noisy when it is overhead. Secure any loose gear that may be blown around. Never fire any flares as the helicopter approaches.

By facing into the wind the helicopter will be able to maximize airflow into its engines. Also, more of the rotor prop-wash will be blown astern of you. If you steer a steady course 30°–40° to starboard of the wind direction, the winchman and pilot will be on the starboard side of the helicopter with a good view of your craft.

WIND

30°–40°

If you have no sails or power, stream out a drogue to keep your bow pointing into the wind.
If you are running before the wind in high winds with big waves and cannot turn round, it is possible for the helicopter to fly backwards and execute a fore-deck pick up. Keep the helicopter informed of all changes in your situation. They have done this hundreds of times in training exercises and for real. They are the experts so listen to them and don't panic.

Methods may vary depending on the country and organisation. Some lower rescue cages and some recommend reefing rather than lowering the mainsail.

# Raising the Alarm

### VHF VOICE CALL
Use VHF to alert the coastguard and other vessels in your area. You must tell them:

- your boat's name
- your position
- how many people are on board
- what assistance you require

VHF is better than a mobile phone for distress calling. Other vessels in your area will hear your call and the coastguard can use VHF transmissions to fix your position.

A mobile phone will only tell one person that you are in trouble. The network coverage is patchy away from land and you won't be able to talk directly to a helicopter or lifeboat.

### DIGITAL VHF (DSC) CALL
You may not have time to send a voice call but some modern VHF sets can:

- send a distress alert or urgency call at the press of a button
- be linked to a GPS to give your position

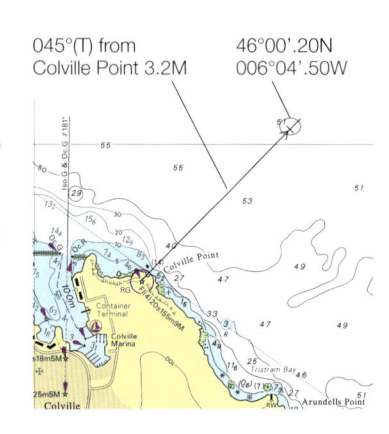

045°(T) from Colville Point 3.2M
46°00'.20N 006°04'.50W

## MAYDAY

When life or vessel are in grave and imminent danger.

Mayday x 3

This is... (yacht name spoken three times and call sign)

(If you have DSC say your MMSI number)

Mayday... (Yacht name, call sign and MMSI number again)

Position is... (Give position in either latitude and longitude or distance and bearing from a charted object)

Nature of Distress (Describe briefly what the problem is, for example sinking, MOB, boat on fire, stranded)

I require immediate assistance

Number of people on board (including yourself)

Further information (Anything that may help rescuers, such as abandoning to liferaft, triggered EPIRB, etc.)

Over (the invitation to reply)

## PAN PAN

Urgency message – if crew or vessel needs assistance.

Pan Pan (Three times)

All stations (Three times)

This is... (name of boat x 3 (+MMSI if fitted with DSC))

Position is... (Give position in latitude and longitude or distance and bearing from a charted object)

Nature of problem (e.g. broken down and in need of a tow)

Number of persons on board (including yourself)

Over

You may use a VHF radio under the supervision of a qualified person or to make a distress call – otherwise you need an operator's certificate.
Contact the RYA or your national maritime authority for details of courses.

Raising the Alarm

## FLARES

Never fire a parachute rocket if a helicopter is approaching.

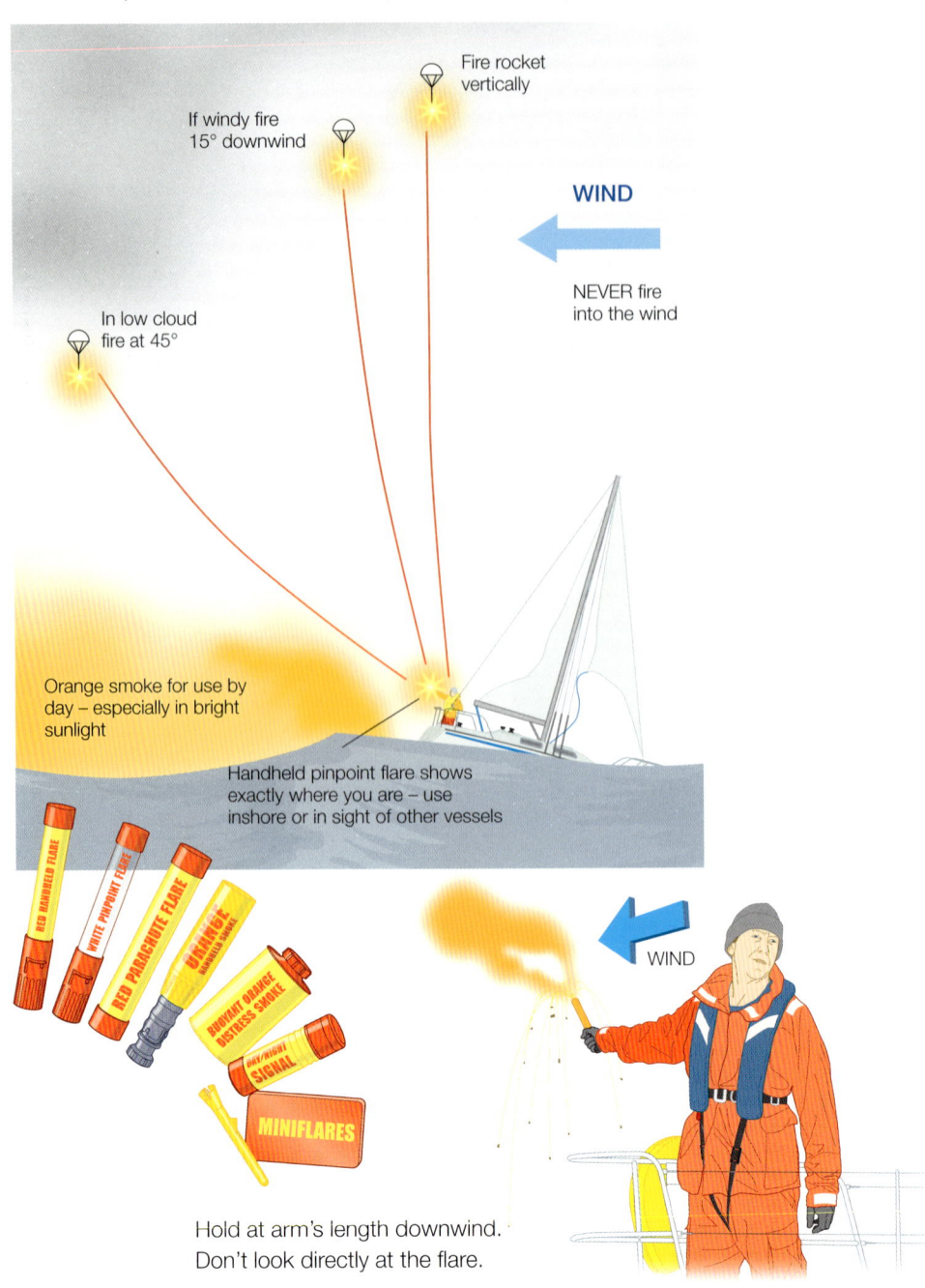

Fire rocket vertically

If windy fire 15° downwind

**WIND**

NEVER fire into the wind

In low cloud fire at 45°

Orange smoke for use by day – especially in bright sunlight

Handheld pinpoint flare shows exactly where you are – use inshore or in sight of other vessels

WIND

Hold at arm's length downwind.
Don't look directly at the flare.

[ 54 ]

Raising the Alarm

## Other Distress Signals

Raising and lowering arms.

Fly a ball over a square.

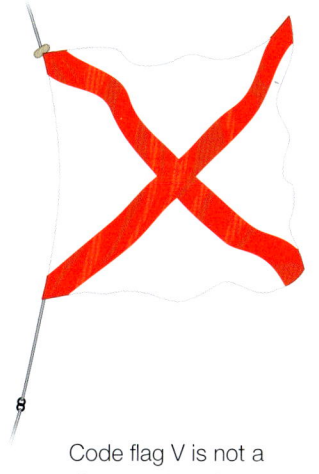

Code flag V is not a distress signal but means 'I require assistance.'

Continuous sounding of the fog horn.

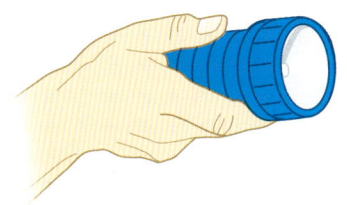

SOS by any means.

[ 55 ]

Rules of the Road

# Rules of the Road

A proper lookout by sight and sound should be kept at all times.

Proceed at a safe speed and beware of faster vessels overtaking.

Beware of blind spots caused by sails/sprayhoods/dodgers etc.

### How can we tell if a risk of Collision Exists?

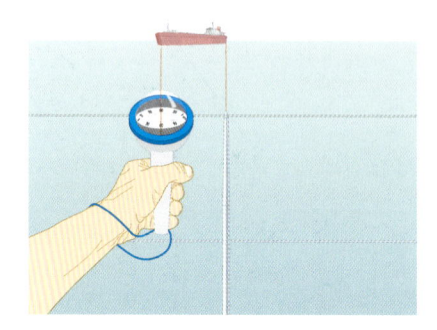

While on a steady course, take a bearing of the ship or line it up with a part of your boat/vessel such as a stanchion or stay.

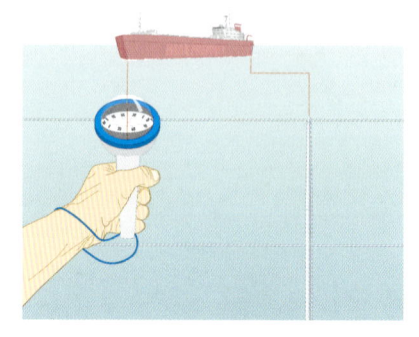

If the bearing of the ship changes or moves in relation to your stanchion there will not be a collision.

If the bearing stays steady or the ship remains lined up with your stanchion, a risk of collision exists.

Rules of the Road

## WHO GIVES WAY?

### Head-on Situation

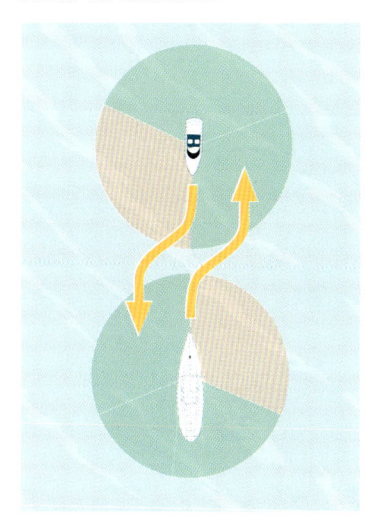

Both vessels turn to starboard.

### Crossing Situation

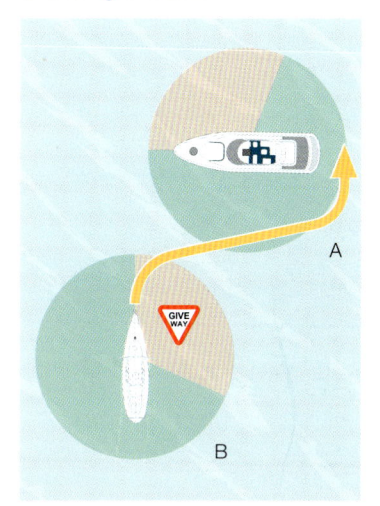

A is on the starboard side of B. B gives way to A.

### Overtaking Situation

Stand-on vessels must keep a steady course and speed.

Any vessel (power or sail) in this sector must give way to the vessel being overtaken.

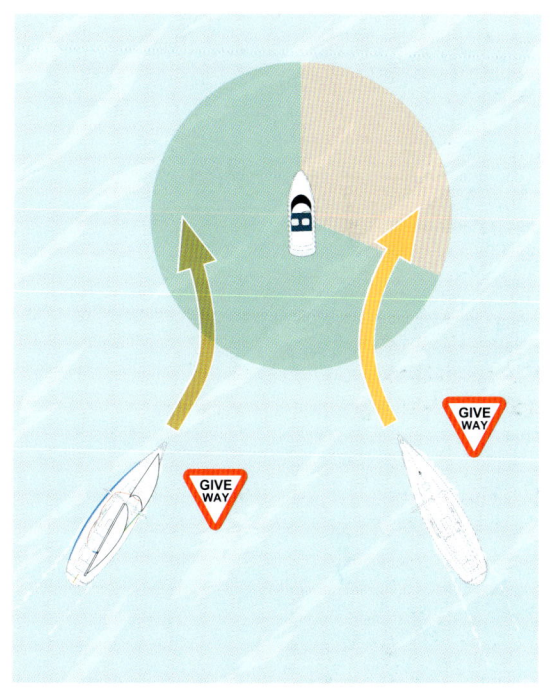

Give-way vessels must make their intentions clear by making an early, bold alteration of course.

[ 57 ]

Rules of the Road

## SAILING VESSELS

### Port/Starboard Situation

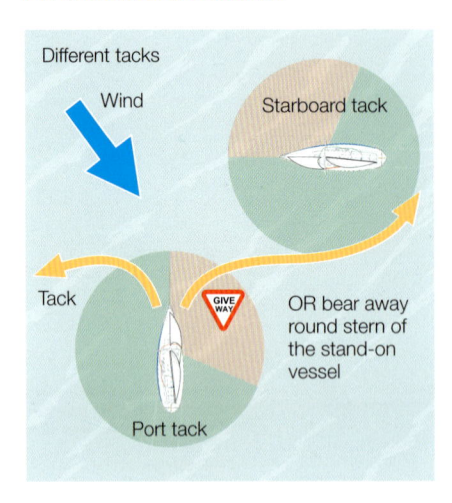

Different tacks
Wind
Starboard tack
Tack
OR bear away round stern of the stand-on vessel
Port tack

Port tack always keeps clear whatever the point of sailing, or must bear away round stern of stand-on vessel.

### Yachts on same tack

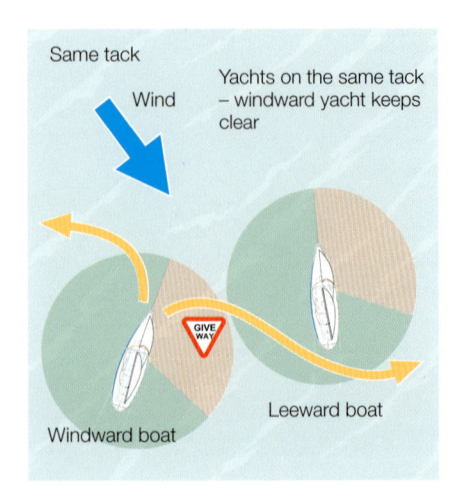

Same tack
Wind
Yachts on the same tack – windward yacht keeps clear
Windward boat
Leeward boat

## SOUND SIGNALS

**In fog**

Vessel under sail, making way

— • •

Power-driven vessel, making way

—

**In sight of each other**

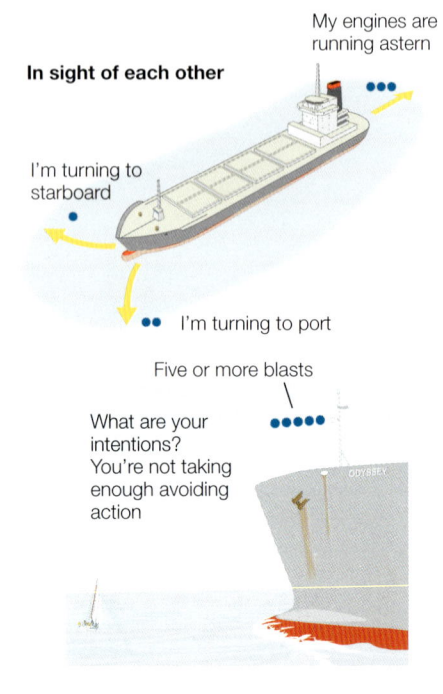

I'm turning to starboard
•

My engines are running astern
• • •

I'm turning to port
• •

Five or more blasts
• • • • •

What are your intentions? You're not taking enough avoiding action

Rules of the Road

## NARROW CHANNELS

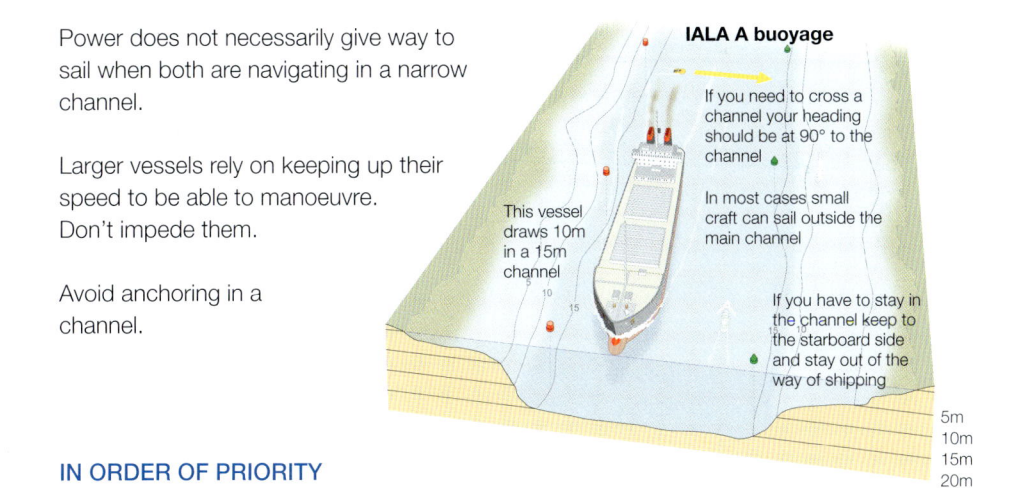

Power does not necessarily give way to sail when both are navigating in a narrow channel.

Larger vessels rely on keeping up their speed to be able to manoeuvre. Don't impede them.

Avoid anchoring in a channel.

**IALA A buoyage**

If you need to cross a channel your heading should be at 90° to the channel

This vessel draws 10m in a 15m channel

In most cases small craft can sail outside the main channel

If you have to stay in the channel keep to the starboard side and stay out of the way of shipping

5m
10m
15m
20m

## IN ORDER OF PRIORITY

The International Regulations for the Prevention of Collisions at Sea (IRPCS) is mostly common sense – a more manoeuvrable vessel must not impede a less manoeuvrable one.

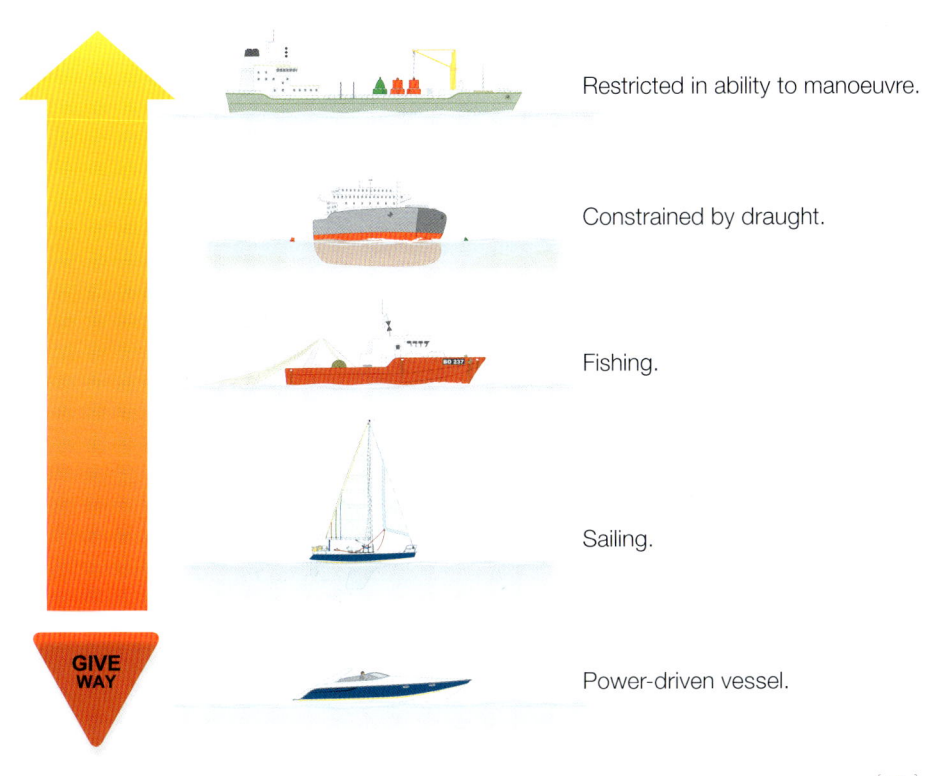

Restricted in ability to manoeuvre.

Constrained by draught.

Fishing.

Sailing.

Power-driven vessel.

**GIVE WAY**

# Lights and Shapes

## UNDER SAIL

### Less than 20m

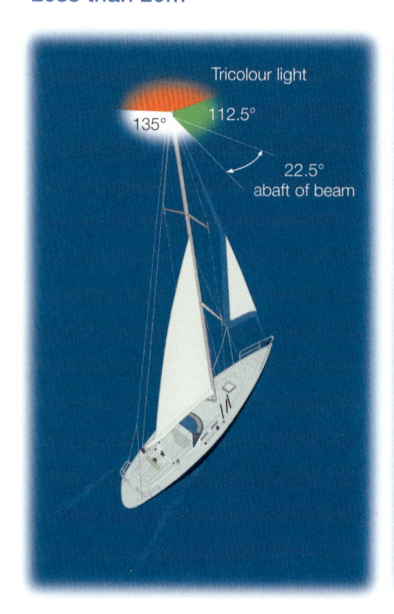

## POWER-DRIVEN VESSELS

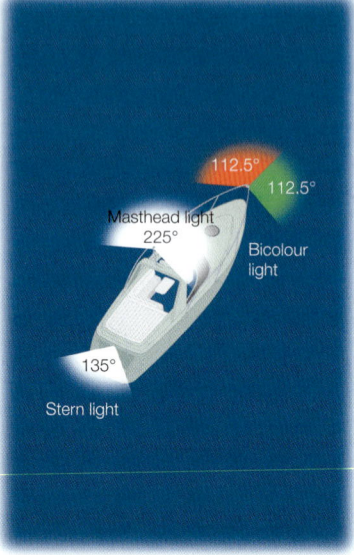

Lights and Shapes

## SAILING VESSEL UNDER POWER

### By Day

▶ Motoring cone

### At Night

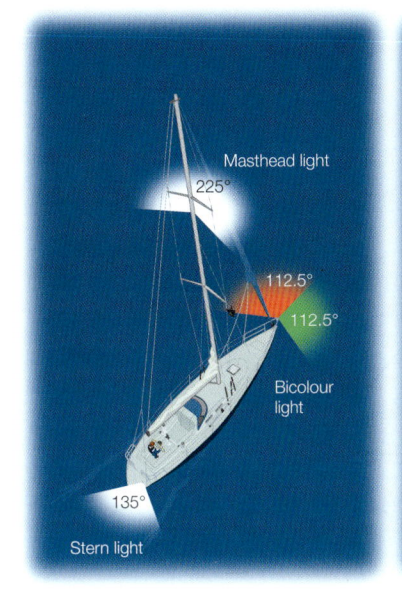

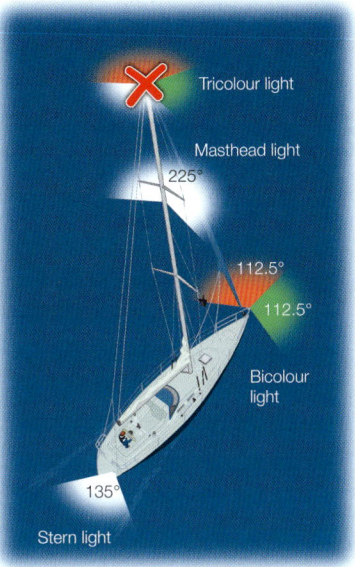

Masthead light 225°
112.5°
112.5°
Bicolour light
135°
Stern light

Tricolour light
Masthead light 225°
112.5°
112.5°
Bicolour light
135°
Stern light

[61]

Lights and Shapes

Larger ships (over 50m) must have two masthead lights.

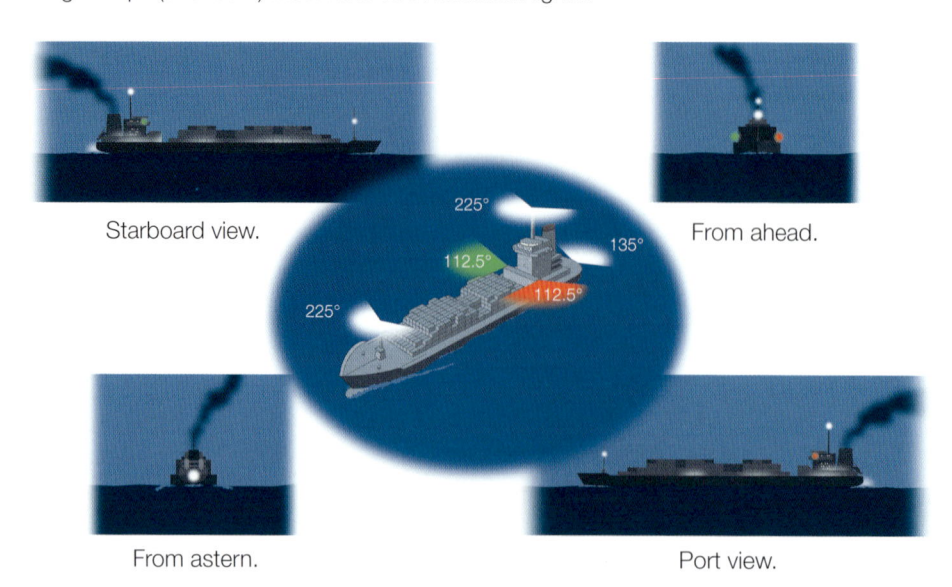

Starboard view.

225°
112.5°
135°
112.5°
225°

From ahead.

From astern.

Port view.

For a full explanation of collision regulations see the book G2 RYA International Regulations for Preventing Collisions at Sea.

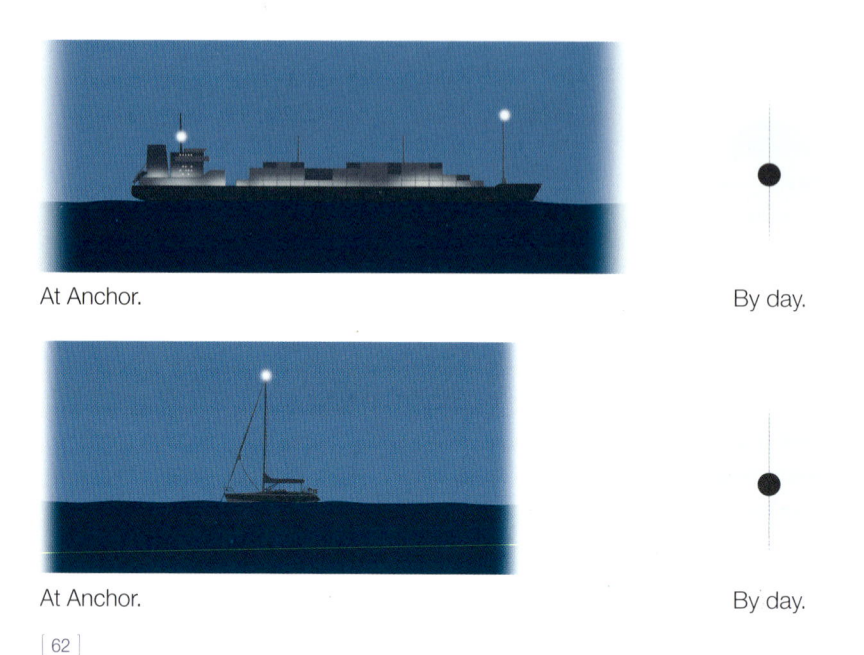

At Anchor.

By day.

At Anchor.

By day.

Lights and Shapes

By day.

Restricted in ability to manoeuvre.

E.g. dredging, cable laying etc

By day.

Carrying out underwater work.

3 all-round reds

E.g. large container ships or tankers in a narrow channel

By day.

Constrained by draught.

By day.

Fishing by trawling.

By day.

Other types of fishing.

[ 63 ]

Lights and Shapes

By day.

White lights have same sector as masthead lights

Towing – over 200m.

By day.

Towing – from astern.

Towing – under 200m.

White lights have same sector as masthead lights

Minesweeping.

By day.

Air cushion vessel.

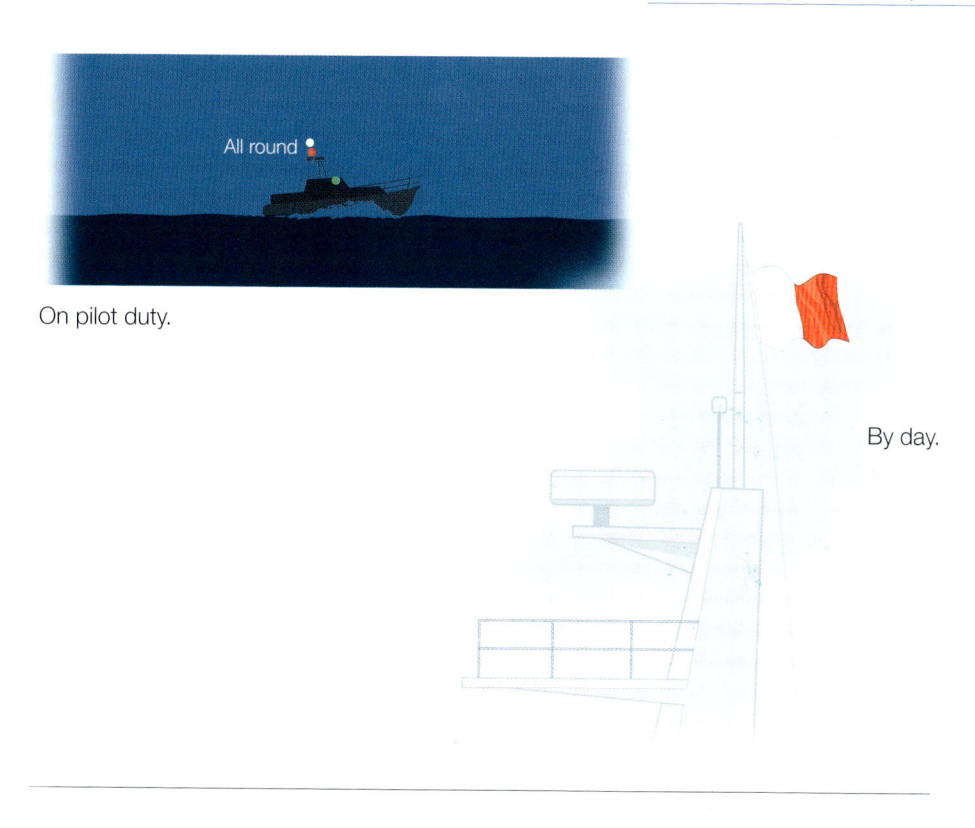

Lights and Shapes

All round

On pilot duty.

By day.

Diving.

By day.

[ 65 ]

# Chart Features

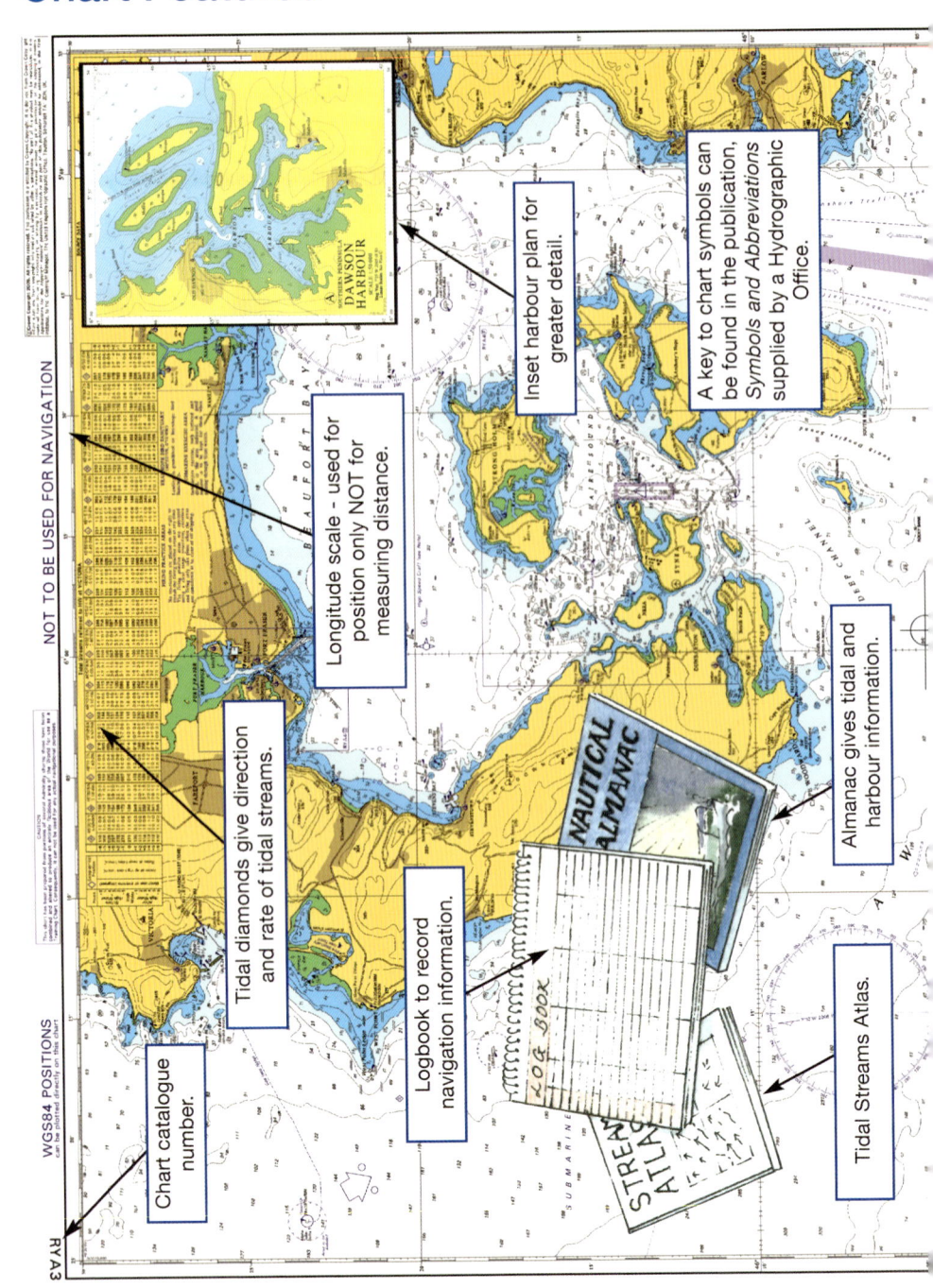

- Inset harbour plan for greater detail.
- A key to chart symbols can be found in the publication, *Symbols and Abbreviations* supplied by a Hydrographic Office.
- Longitude scale - used for position only NOT for measuring distance.
- Almanac gives tidal and harbour information.
- Tidal diamonds give direction and rate of tidal streams.
- Logbook to record navigation information.
- Tidal Streams Atlas.
- Chart catalogue number.

Chart Features

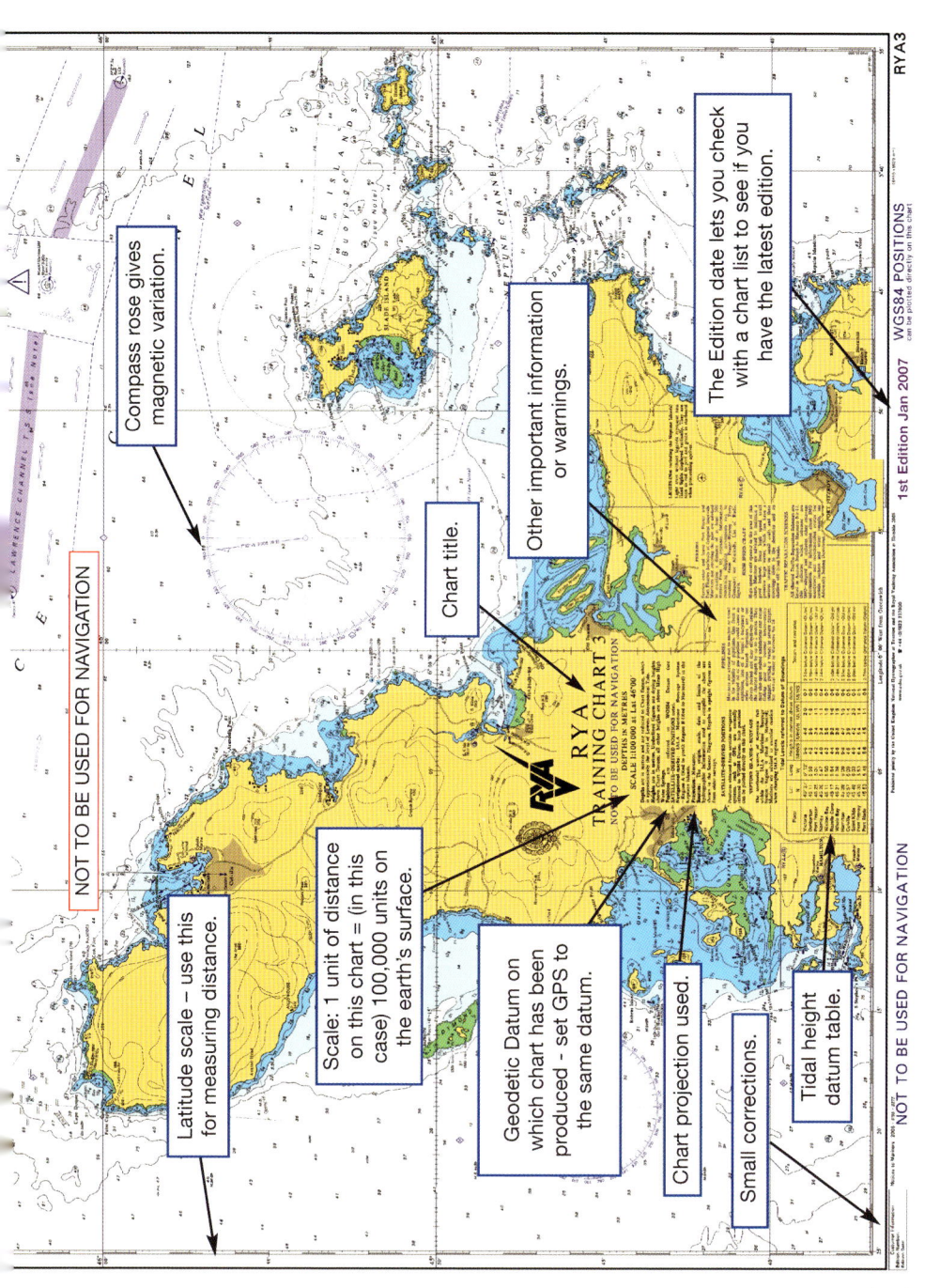

- Compass rose gives magnetic variation.
- Other important information or warnings.
- The Edition date lets you check with a chart list to see if you have the latest edition.
- Chart title.
- Latitude scale – use this for measuring distance.
- Scale: 1 unit of distance on this chart = (in this case) 100,000 units on the earth's surface.
- Geodetic Datum on which chart has been produced – set GPS to the same datum.
- Chart projection used.
- Small corrections.
- Tidal height datum table.

NOT TO BE USED FOR NAVIGATION

1st Edition Jan 2007

WGS84 POSITIONS can be plotted directly on this chart

RYA3

[ 67 ]

Interpreting Charts

# Interpreting Charts

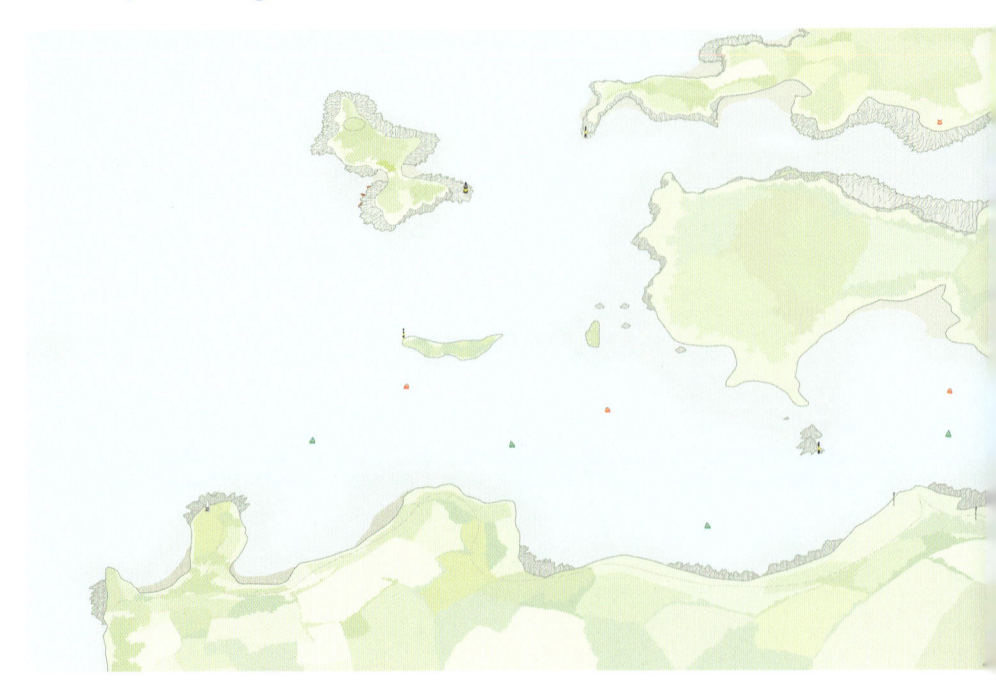

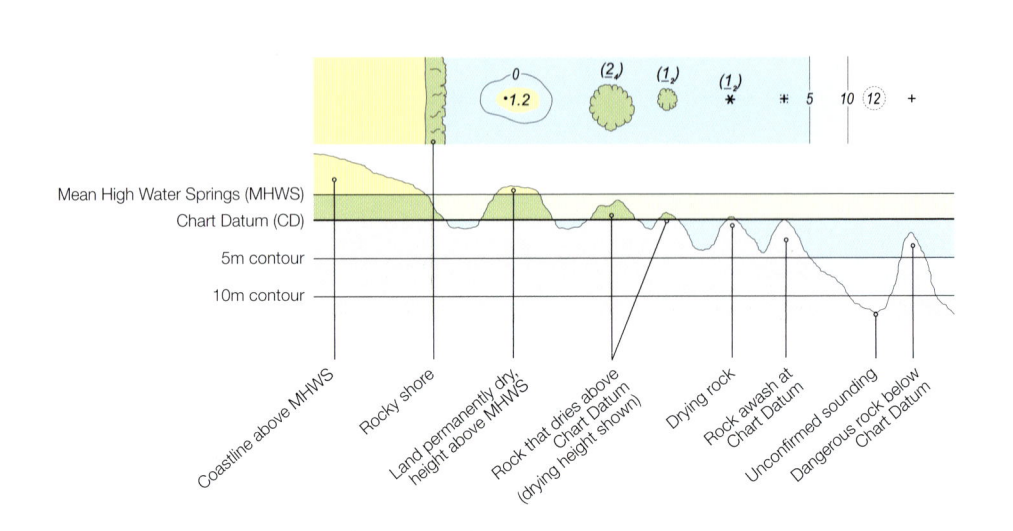

Mean High Water Springs (MHWS)
Chart Datum (CD)
5m contour
10m contour

Coastline above MHWS
Rocky shore
Land permanently dry, height above MHWS
Rock that dries above Chart Datum (drying height shown)
Drying rock
Rock awash at Chart Datum
Unconfirmed sounding
Dangerous rock below Chart Datum

[ 68 ]

# Interpreting Charts

Like land maps, charts use symbols to show useful and important features. Information is chosen carefully to show hazards clearly and to help identify features that are visible from a boat at sea.

Symbols and abbreviations published by a hydrographic office can be used to identify features and symbols on the chart (IALA A Buoyage).

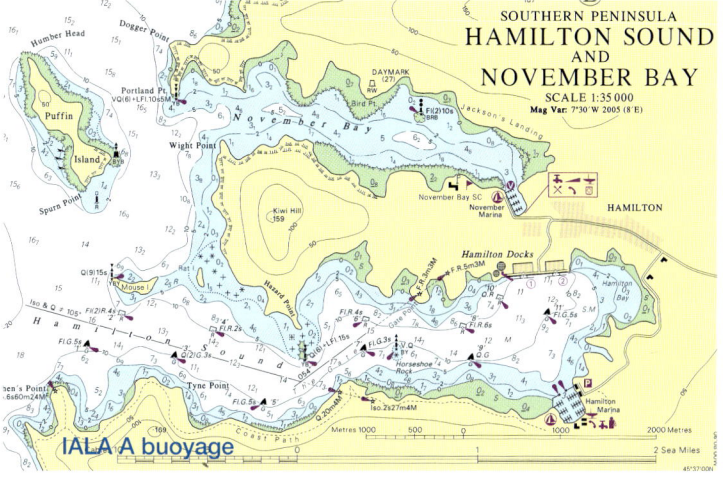

IALA A buoyage

| | | |
|---|---|---|
| Beacon | Wreck, depth unknown, not considered dangerous to surface navigation | Chimney |
| Yacht harbour/marina | | Steep coast, cliffs |
| Can buoy | Battery, small fort | Building |

[ 69 ]

# Plotting your Position

## BY LATITUDE AND LONGITUDE

Lines of longitude run from pole to pole dividing the earth into segments, rather like an orange.

Lines of latitude are obtained by projecting angles made from the centre of the earth to points on its surface.

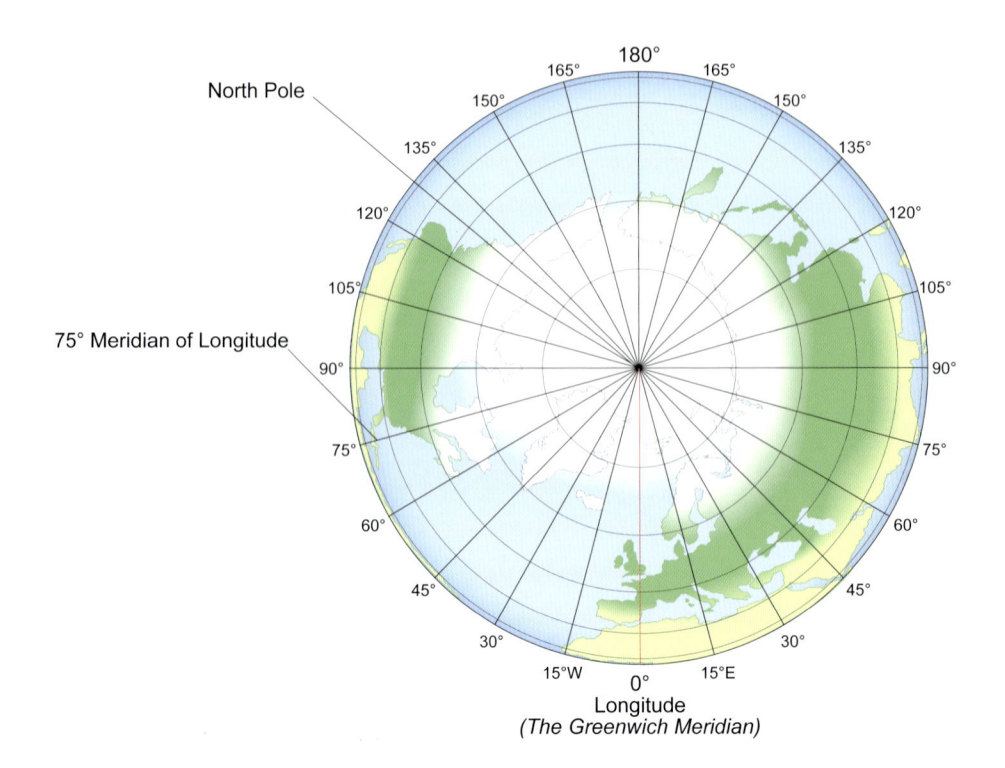

Plotting your Position

## Distance and Speed
For all practical purposes a mile at sea is 1852 metres.

1° (degree) = 60' (minutes) of latitude

1' (minute) = 1 nautical mile

Speed is measured in knots. A knot is one nautical mile per hour.

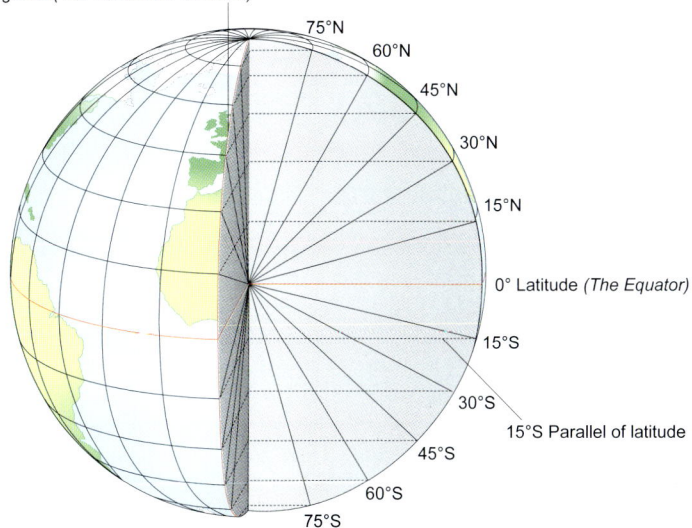

0° Longitude *(The Greenwich Meridian)*
75°N
60°N
45°N
30°N
15°N
0° Latitude *(The Equator)*
15°S
30°S
15°S Parallel of latitude
45°S
60°S
75°S

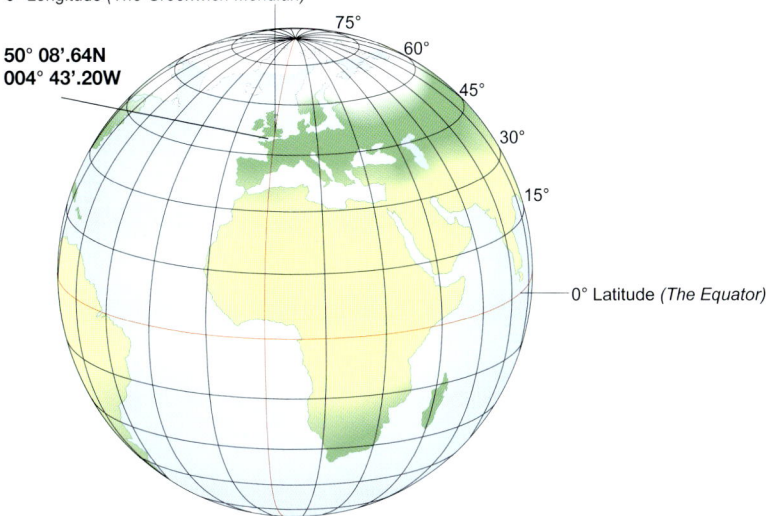

0° Longitude *(The Greenwich Meridian)*
**50° 08'.64N**
**004° 43'.20W**
75°
60°
45°
30°
15°
0° Latitude *(The Equator)*

Plotting your Position

## Plotting Position

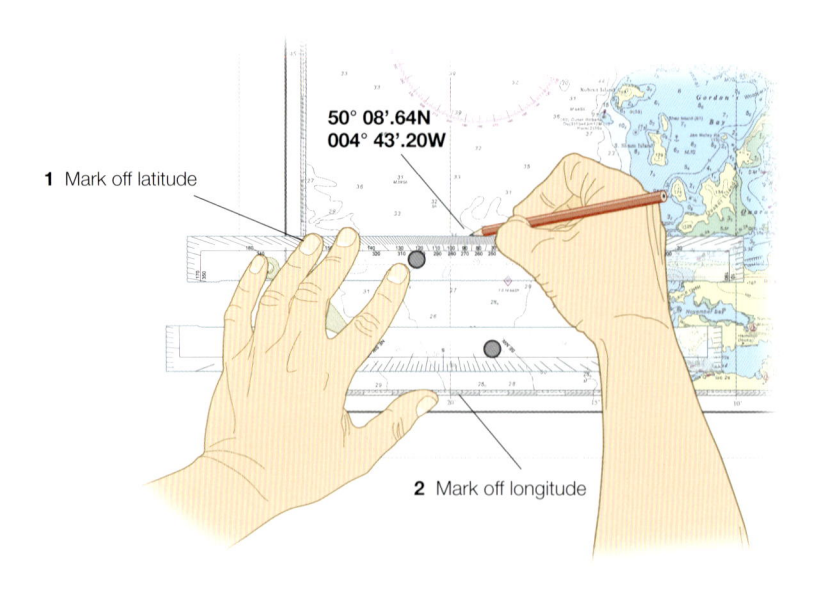

50° 08'.64N
004° 43'.20W

**1** Mark off latitude

**2** Mark off longitude

## WITH A PLOTTER
### By Range and Bearing

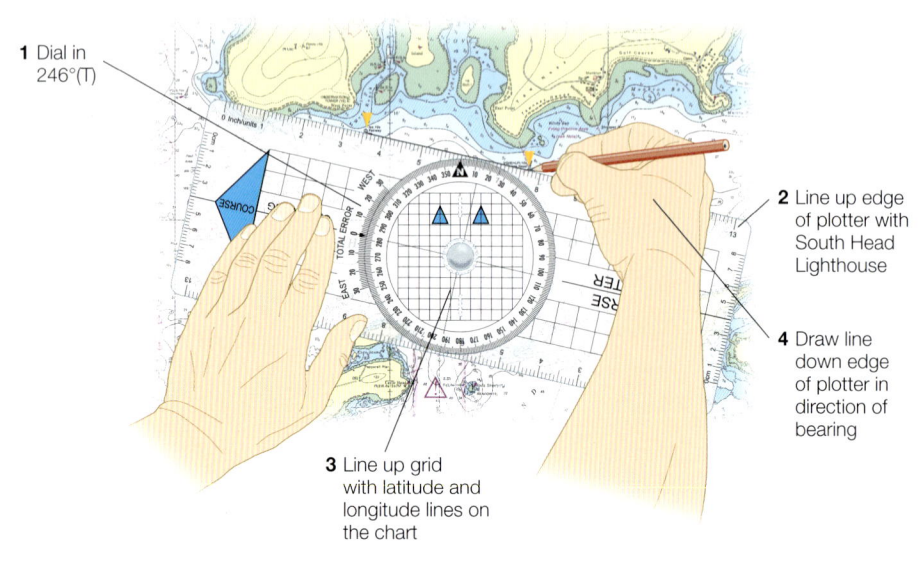

**1** Dial in 246°(T)

**2** Line up edge of plotter with South Head Lighthouse

**3** Line up grid with latitude and longitude lines on the chart

**4** Draw line down edge of plotter in direction of bearing

[ 72 ]

Plotting your Position

## With Parallel Rules

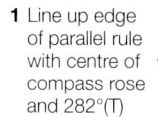

**1** Line up edge of parallel rule with centre of compass rose and 282°(T)

**2** Keeping rules steady, walk them to line up with the Fairway buoy

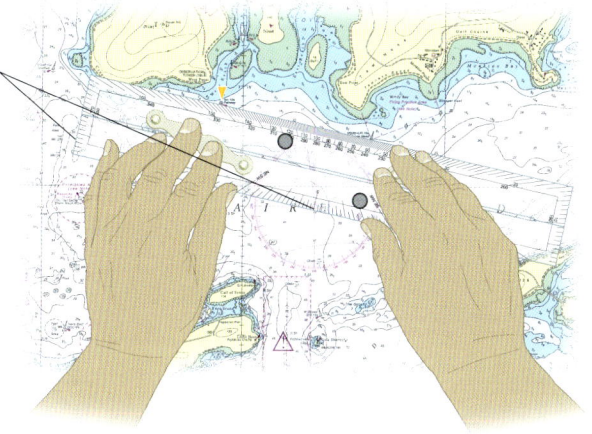

**3** When aligned with the Fairway buoy, draw line down edge of rules in direction of bearing

## Measuring Distance

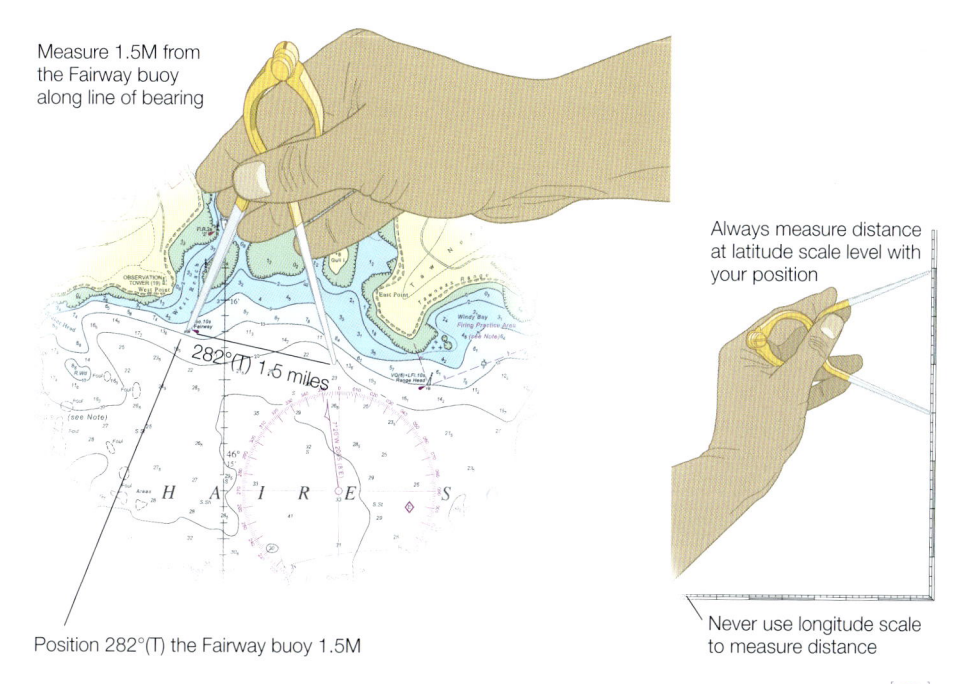

Measure 1.5M from the Fairway buoy along line of bearing

282°(T) 1.5 miles

Position 282°(T) the Fairway buoy 1.5M

Always measure distance at latitude scale level with your position

Never use longitude scale to measure distance

[ 73 ]

# Variation

Charts show North as True (geographic) North. A compass can only point to Magnetic North, which changes with time and according to your position.

The difference between True and Magnetic North is called variation.

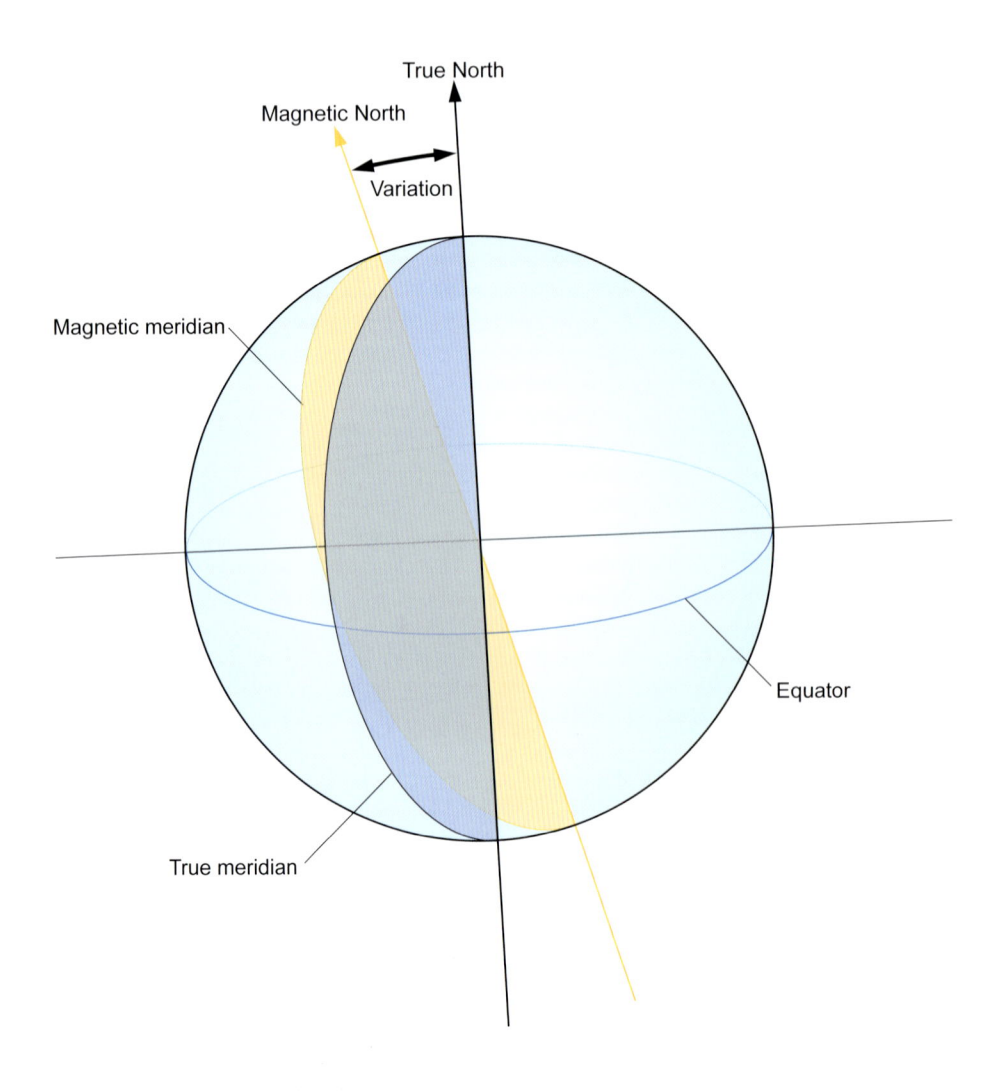

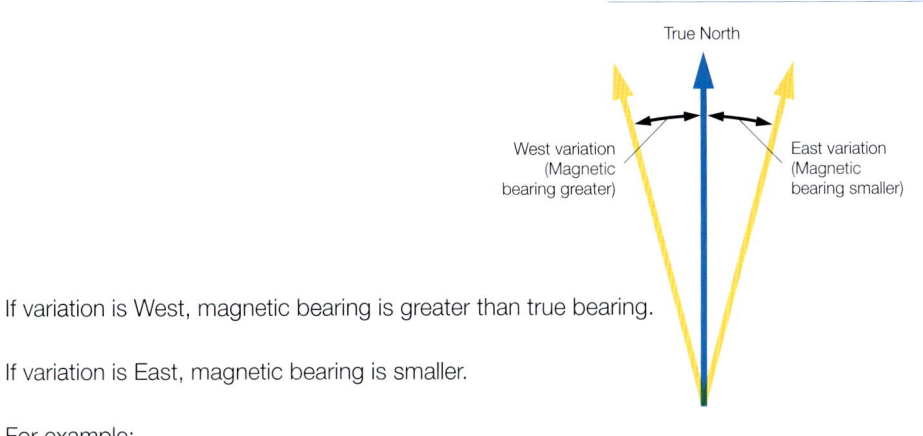

# Variation

If variation is West, magnetic bearing is greater than true bearing.

If variation is East, magnetic bearing is smaller.

For example:
With 5 degrees West variation: 070 degrees (T) = 075 degrees (M)
With 5 degrees East variation: 070 degrees (T) = 065 degrees (M)

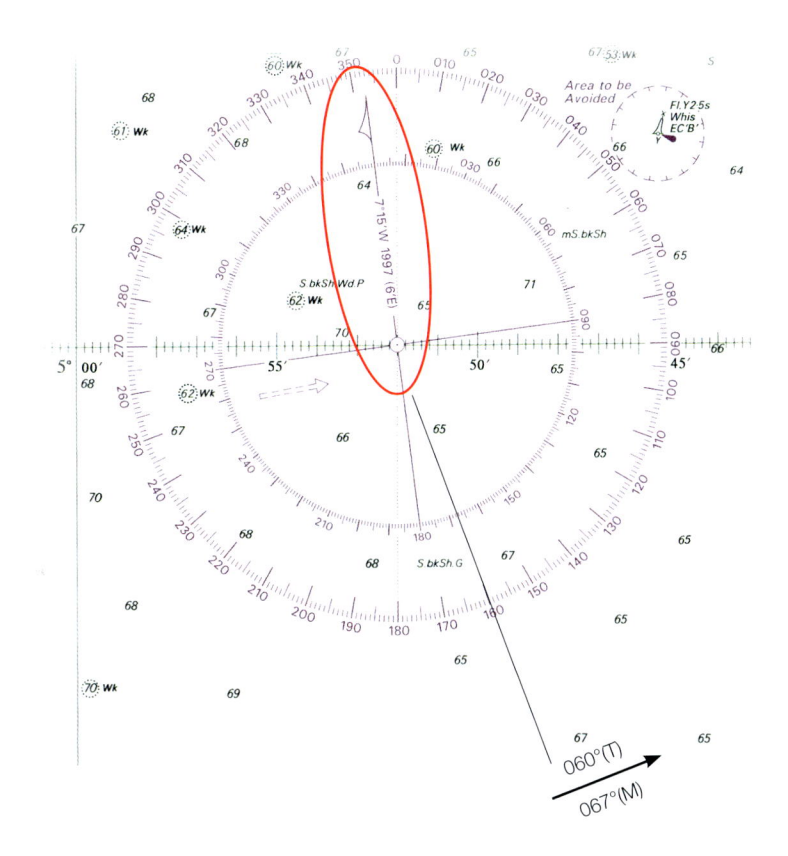

Variation for your position is found on the nearest compass rose.

[75]

# Deviation

Deviation is caused by ferrous metals and electromagnetic fields on board which will affect the accuracy of the compass.

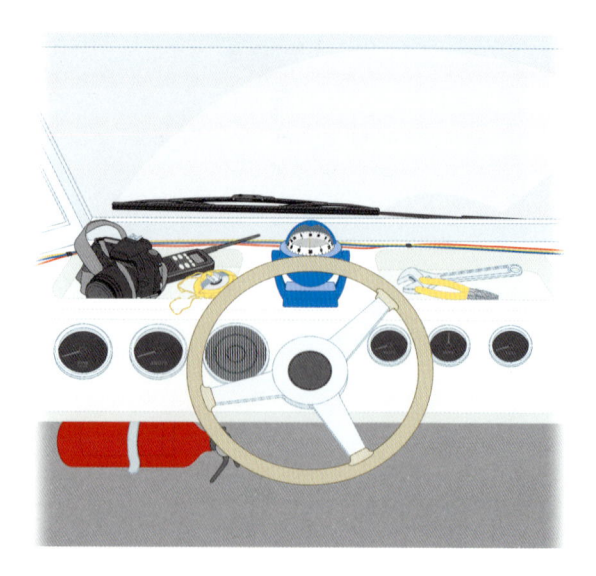

The ship's compass is swung to check the effect of magnetic influences on board. This will vary as the boat's heading changes. A card can be produced for your steering compass showing the deviation for each heading.

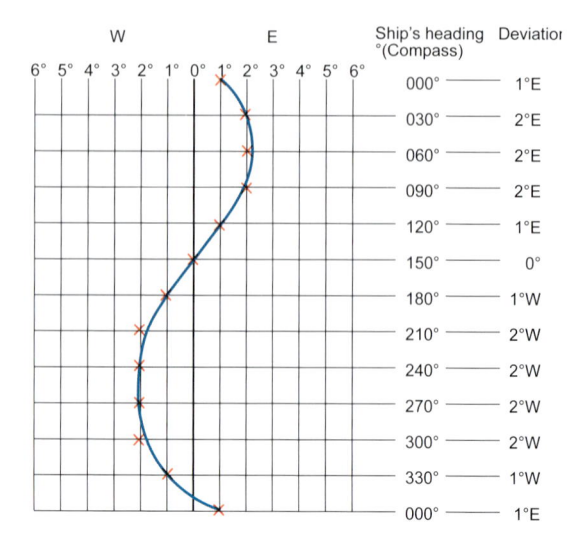

| Ship's heading °(Compass) | Deviation |
|---|---|
| 000° | 1°E |
| 030° | 2°E |
| 060° | 2°E |
| 090° | 2°E |
| 120° | 1°E |
| 150° | 0° |
| 180° | 1°W |
| 210° | 2°W |
| 240° | 2°W |
| 270° | 2°W |
| 300° | 2°W |
| 330° | 1°W |
| 000° | 1°E |

# Deviation

## How to Apply Variation and Deviation

Chartwork is in degrees True. Compass courses must be in degrees Compass.

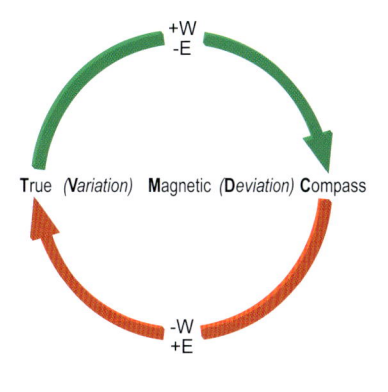

+W
-E

True *(Variation)* Magnetic *(Deviation)* Compass

-W
+E

## Finding a Compass Course

True bearing from chart 060°(T)
Variation +7°W
Magnetic bearing = 067°(M)
Apply deviation from card -2°E
Compass course = 065°(C)

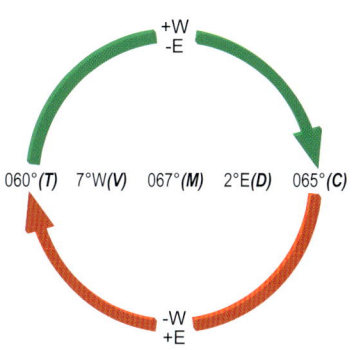

+W
-E

060°*(T)* 7°W*(V)* 067°*(M)* 2°E*(D)* 065°*(C)*

-W
+E

## Checking for Deviation

Point the boat straight at a transit and compare results.

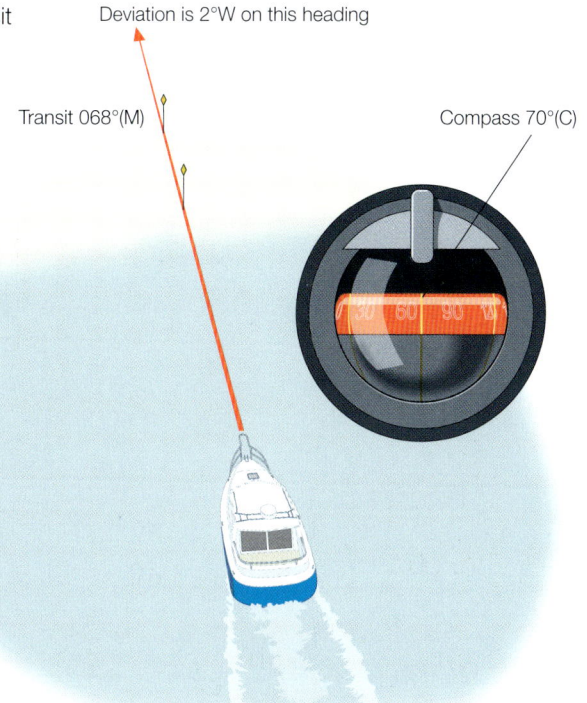

Deviation is 2°W on this heading

Transit 068°(M)

Compass 70°(C)

[ 77 ]

# Tidal Theory

## TIDES

The gravitational pull of the moon and sun is the main cause of tides.

Moon and sun in line – spring tides.

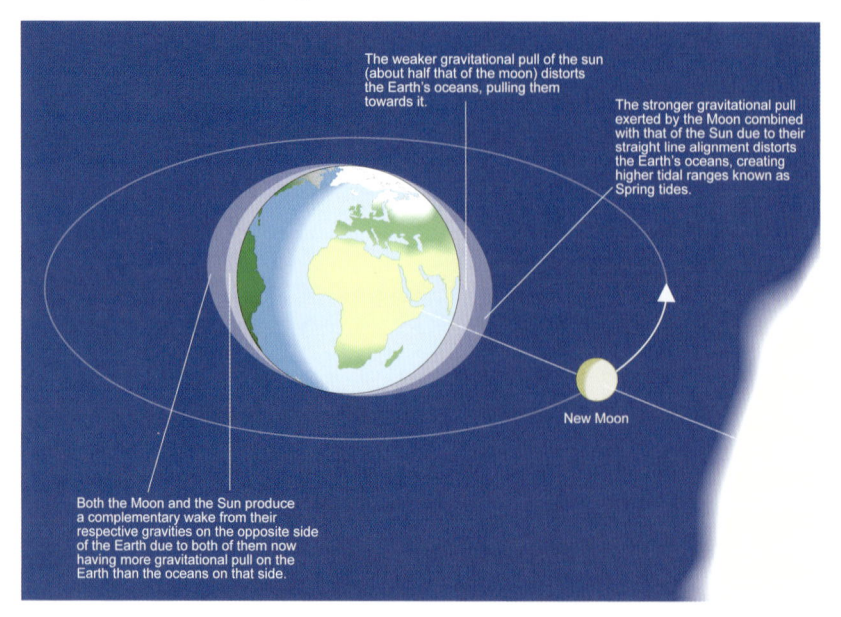

The weaker gravitational pull of the sun (about half that of the moon) distorts the Earth's oceans, pulling them towards it.

The stronger gravitational pull exerted by the Moon combined with that of the Sun due to their straight line alignment distorts the Earth's oceans, creating higher tidal ranges known as Spring tides.

New Moon

Both the Moon and the Sun produce a complementary wake from their respective gravities on the opposite side of the Earth due to both of them now having more gravitational pull on the Earth than the oceans on that side.

Moon and sun opposing – neap tides.

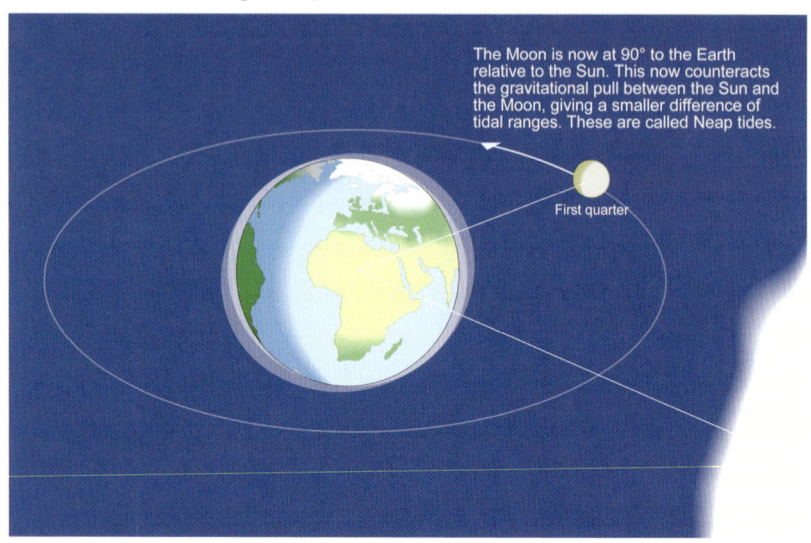

The Moon is now at 90° to the Earth relative to the Sun. This now counteracts the gravitational pull between the Sun and the Moon, giving a smaller difference of tidal ranges. These are called Neap tides.

First quarter

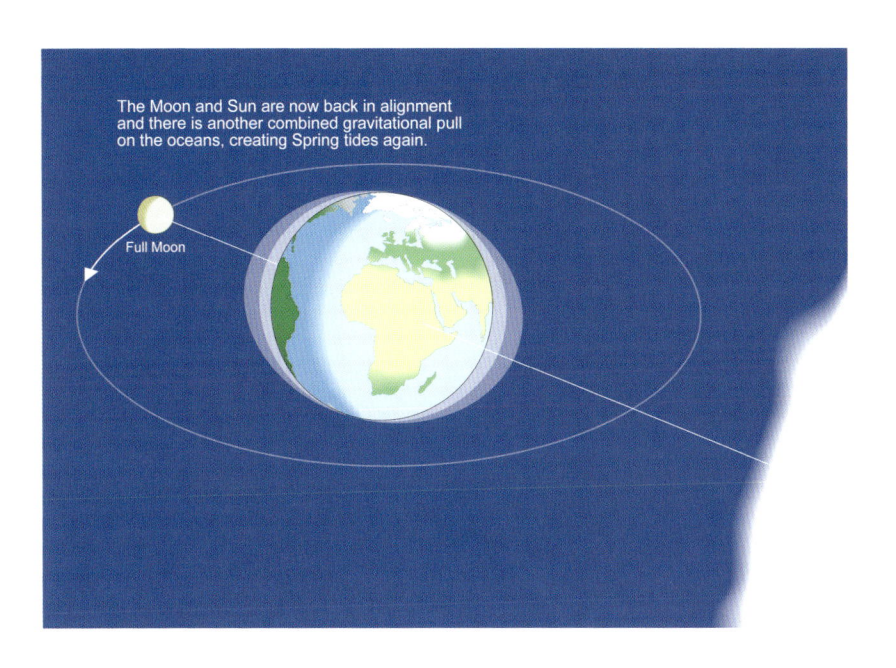

# Tidal Theory

The Moon and Sun are now back in alignment and there is another combined gravitational pull on the oceans, creating Spring tides again.

Full Moon

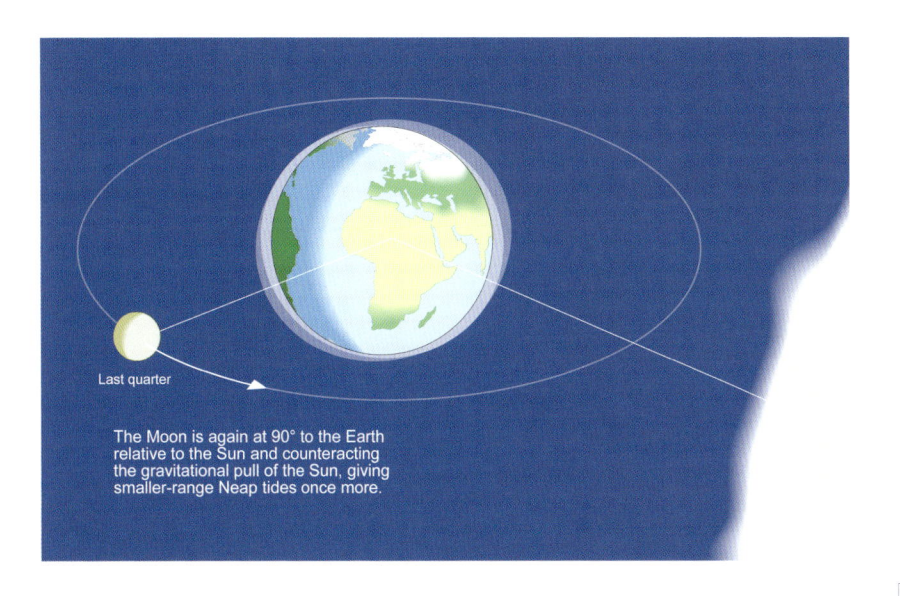

Last quarter

The Moon is again at 90° to the Earth relative to the Sun and counteracting the gravitational pull of the Sun, giving smaller-range Neap tides once more.

## Tidal Theory

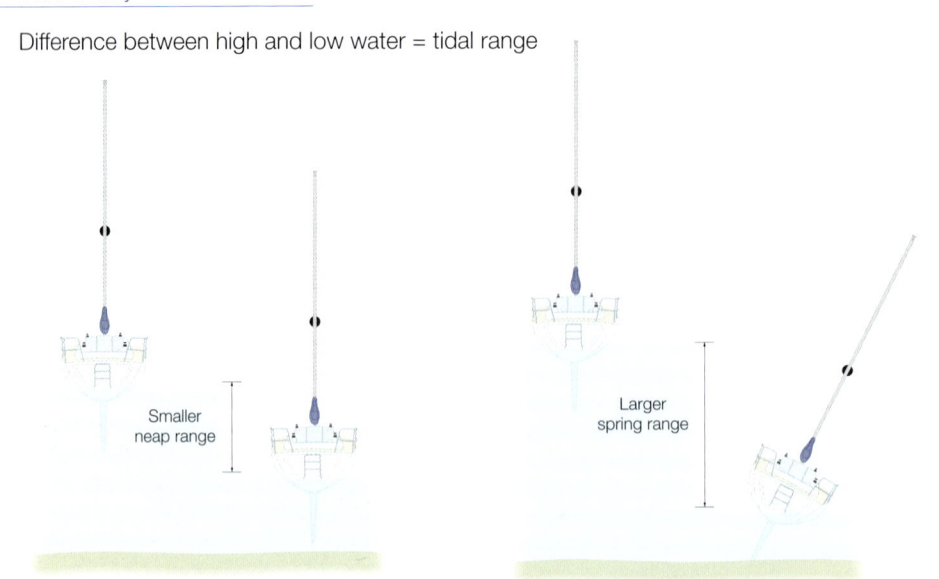

Difference between high and low water = tidal range

Smaller neap range

Larger spring range

## Daily Tides

Each day as the earth rotates we experience two high and two low waters.

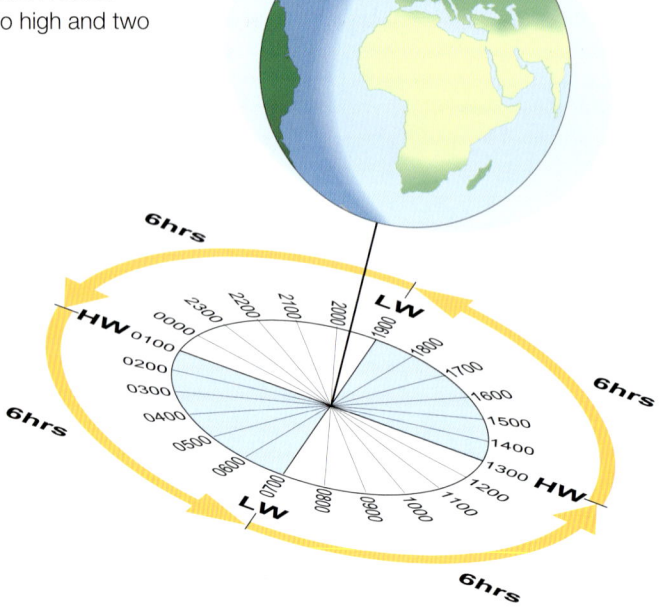

[ 80 ]

# Tidal Theory

## Tidal Terms

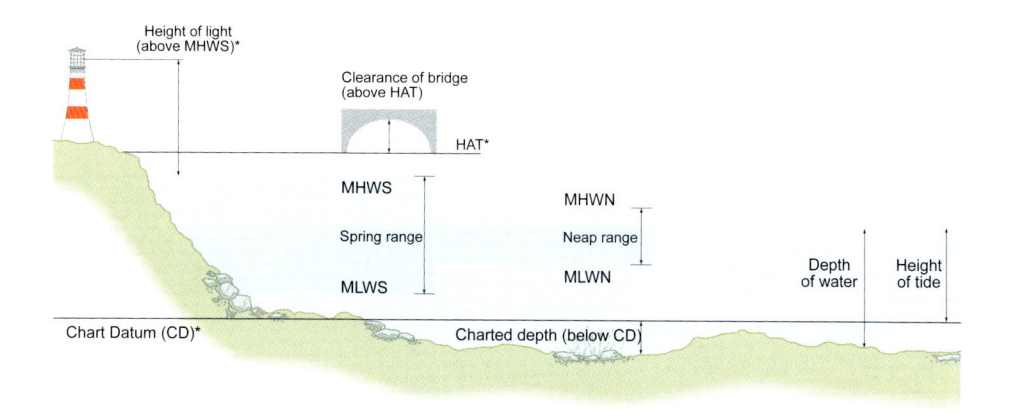

MHWS – Mean High Water Springs    MLWS – Mean Low Water Springs    HAT – Highest Astronomical Tide
MHWN – Mean High Water Neaps     MLWN – Mean Low Water Neaps      CD – Chart Datum

*Specific datums used for heights, clearances and charted depth may vary in different countries. For example, the UK uses lowest astronomical tide for chart datum, whereas the USA uses mean low low water.

Tidal Theory

## HOW MUCH WATER?

The depth of water under your boat is measured with an echo sounder. Ultrasonic signals are transmitted to and reflected from the seabed to give the depth of water on a digital or analogue display.

The transducer is situated below the waterline. Allow for this when reading the display. You can also calibrate for the display to read from waterline or bottom of keel.

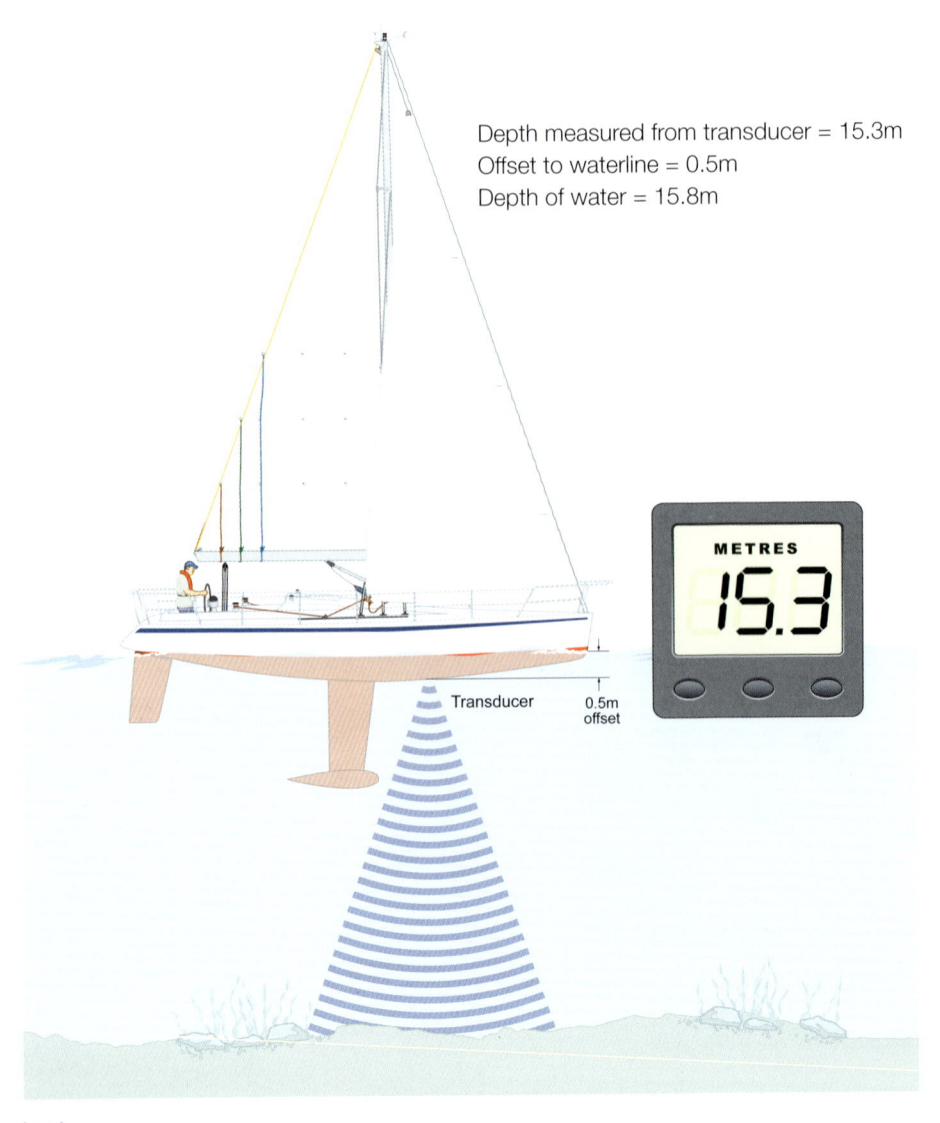

Depth measured from transducer = 15.3m
Offset to waterline = 0.5m
Depth of water = 15.8m

Transducer   0.5m offset

METRES
15.3

# Tidal Theory

A chart shows depths you are likely to meet at the chart datum (CD).

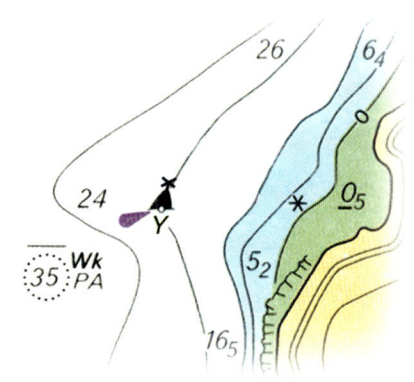

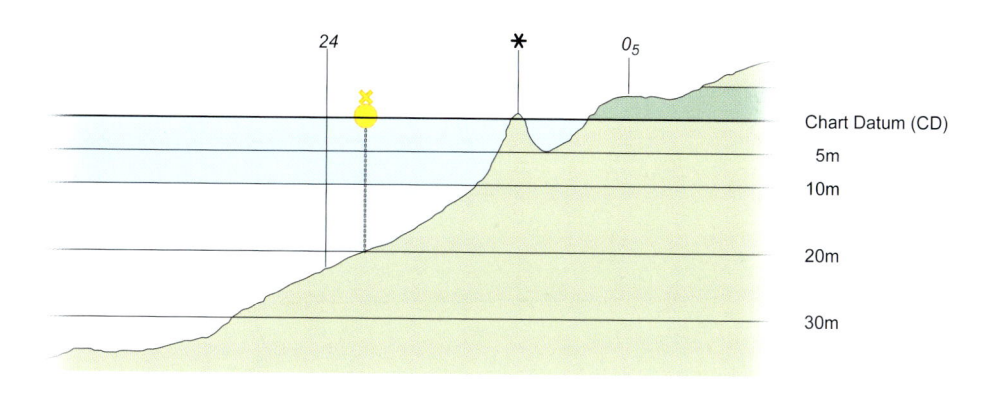

Chart Datum (CD)
5m
10m
20m
30m

[ 83 ]

## Tidal Theory

Height of tide is measured above CD.

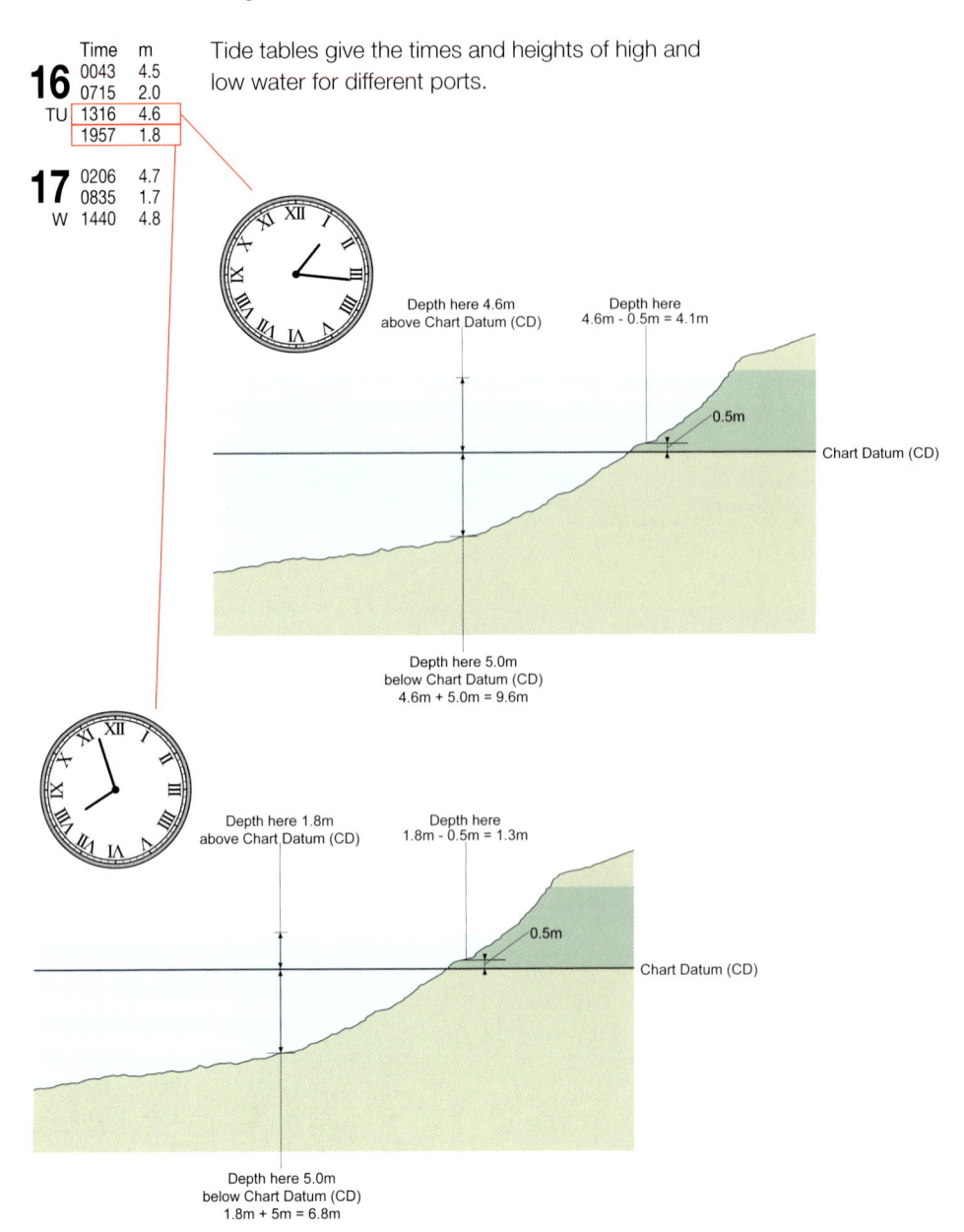

Tide tables give the times and heights of high and low water for different ports.

| | Time | m |
|---|---|---|
| **16** TU | 0043 | 4.5 |
| | 0715 | 2.0 |
| | 1316 | 4.6 |
| | 1957 | 1.8 |
| **17** W | 0206 | 4.7 |
| | 0835 | 1.7 |
| | 1440 | 4.8 |

Depth here 4.6m above Chart Datum (CD)

Depth here 4.6m - 0.5m = 4.1m

0.5m

Chart Datum (CD)

Depth here 5.0m below Chart Datum (CD)
4.6m + 5.0m = 9.6m

Depth here 1.8m above Chart Datum (CD)

Depth here 1.8m - 0.5m = 1.3m

0.5m

Chart Datum (CD)

Depth here 5.0m below Chart Datum (CD)
1.8m + 5m = 6.8m

Add depths below CD to the height of tide.

Subtract drying heights from the height of tide.

## Tidal Theory

### Standard Ports

Tide tables are produced for larger ports and give the times and heights of high and low water for every day of the year. Tide times may need correcting for local changes, such as differences in time zone from Universal Time (UT) and in countries operating Daylight Saving Time (DST) in the summer (BST in the U.K.).

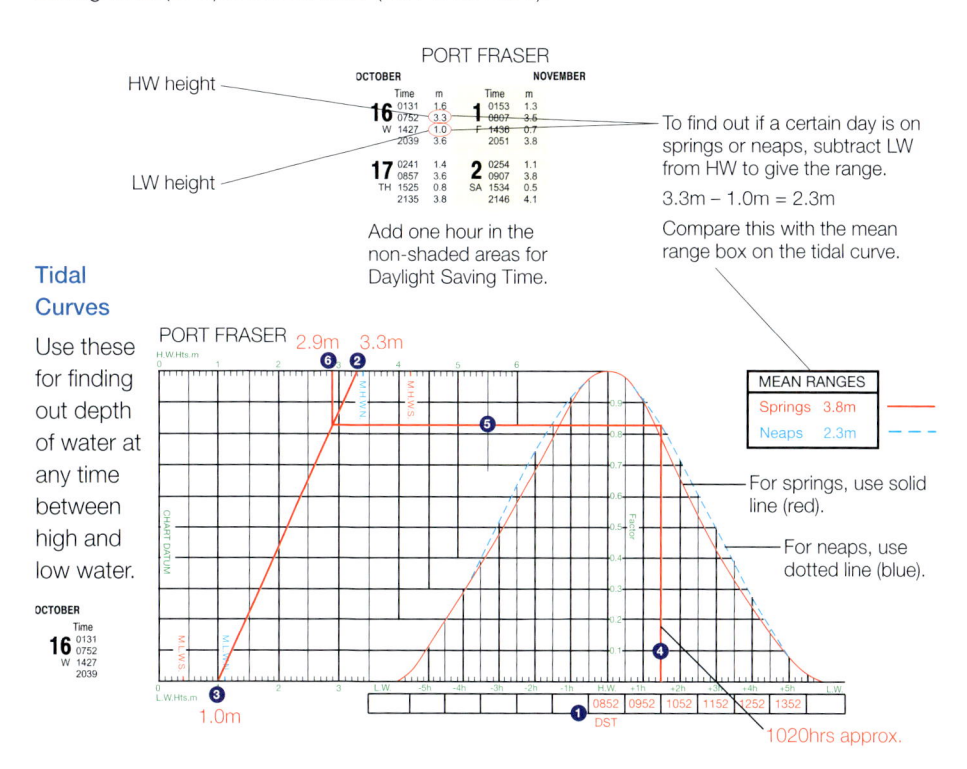

HW height

LW height

**PORT FRASER**

| OCTOBER | | | NOVEMBER | | |
|---|---|---|---|---|---|
| | Time | m | | Time | m |
| **16** | 0131 | 1.6 | **1** | 0153 | 1.3 |
| W | 0752 | 3.3 | F | 0807 | 3.5 |
| | 1427 | 1.0 | | 1436 | 0.7 |
| | 2039 | 3.6 | | 2051 | 3.8 |
| **17** | 0241 | 1.4 | **2** | 0254 | 1.1 |
| TH | 0857 | 3.6 | SA | 0907 | 3.8 |
| | 1525 | 0.8 | | 1534 | 0.5 |
| | 2135 | 3.8 | | 2146 | 4.1 |

Add one hour in the non-shaded areas for Daylight Saving Time.

To find out if a certain day is on springs or neaps, subtract LW from HW to give the range.

3.3m – 1.0m = 2.3m

Compare this with the mean range box on the tidal curve.

### Tidal Curves

Use these for finding out depth of water at any time between high and low water.

**PORT FRASER**  2.9m  3.3m

OCTOBER
Time
**16** 0131
 0752
W 1427
 2039

1.0m

**MEAN RANGES**
Springs 3.8m
Neaps 2.3m

For springs, use solid line (red).

For neaps, use dotted line (blue).

1020hrs approx.

---

What will be the height of tide at Port Fraser at 1020hrs on Wednesday 16 October?

**❶** Enter HW (local time and fill in the boxes for each hour after HW.

**❷ & ❸** Mark in the heights of HW and LW and draw a line between them.

**❹** Find 1020hrs on the bottom scale.

**❺** Draw a line upwards to hit the curve, then across to meet the HW/LW line, and then up to the HW scale (use the neaps curve, as HW minus LW equals 2.3m (neaps)).

**❻** There will be 2.9m at 1020hrs.

You can also find out when there will be a specific depth, e.g. at what time after HW will there be 2.0m of tide?
Go down to the HW/LW line from the HW scale, across to the curve and down to the time scale to find the answer – 1210hrs.

[ 85 ]

## Tidal Theory

### Secondary Ports

Tide tables are not produced for minor ports. To find the height and times of HW and LW at these secondary ports you will need to apply corrections, which are usually found in an almanac, to the times and heights of a standard port nearby.

**Standard Port PORT FRASER ( ← )**

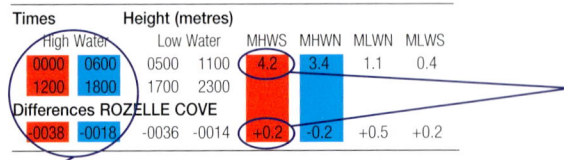

| Times | | Height (metres) | | | | | |
|---|---|---|---|---|---|---|---|
| High Water | | Low Water | | MHWS | MHWN | MLWN | MLWS |
| 0000 | 0600 | 0500 | 1100 | 4.2 | 3.4 | 1.1 | 0.4 |
| 1200 | 1800 | 1700 | 2300 | | | | |
| Differences ROZELLE COVE | | | | | | | |
| -0038 | -0018 | -0036 | -0014 | +0.2 | -0.2 | +0.5 | +0.2 |

Height difference: When HW at Port Fraser is 4.2m it is 0.2m more at Rozelle Cove. When HW is 3.4m, it is 0.2m less at Rozelle Cove.

Time difference: If HW for Port Fraser is at 0000hrs or 1200hrs, HW for Rozelle Cove is 38 minutes earlier, but when HW for Port Fraser is at 0600hrs or 1800hrs HW for Rozelle Cove is 18 minutes earlier.

However, if HW and LW times fall between these set times, you will need to interpolate between the corrections, e.g. if HW at Port Fraser is 0752hrs UT, what time is HW at Rozelle Cove?

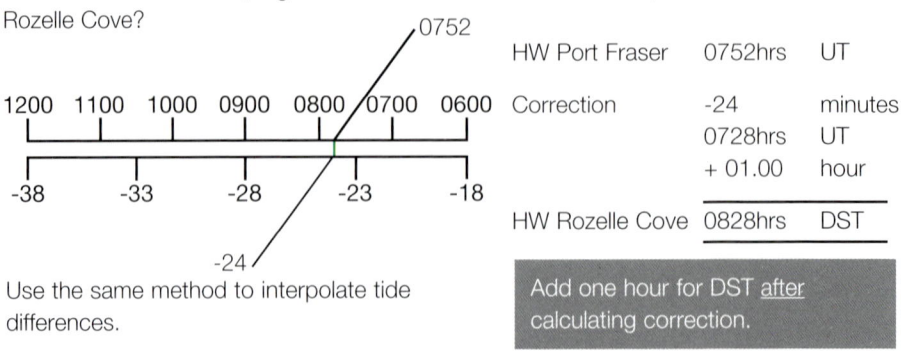

| | | |
|---|---|---|
| HW Port Fraser | 0752hrs | UT |
| Correction | -24 | minutes |
| | 0728hrs | UT |
| | + 01.00 | hour |
| HW Rozelle Cove | 0828hrs | DST |

Use the same method to interpolate tide differences.

*Add one hour for DST after calculating correction.*

To find the height of tide between HW and LW at a secondary port, use the tidal curve for the standard port and the secondary port data.

Use the related standard port.

For example, for Rozelle Cove you should use the curve for Port Fraser.

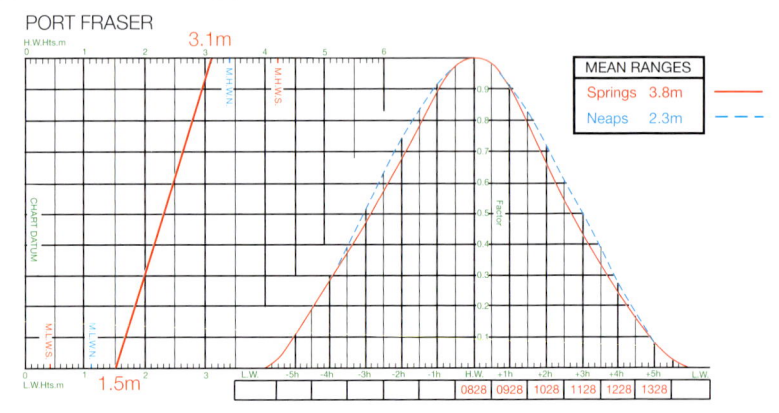

**PORT FRASER**

MEAN RANGES
Springs 3.8m
Neaps 2.3m

[ 86 ]

# Tidal Streams

## Consider the Tide as a Travelator

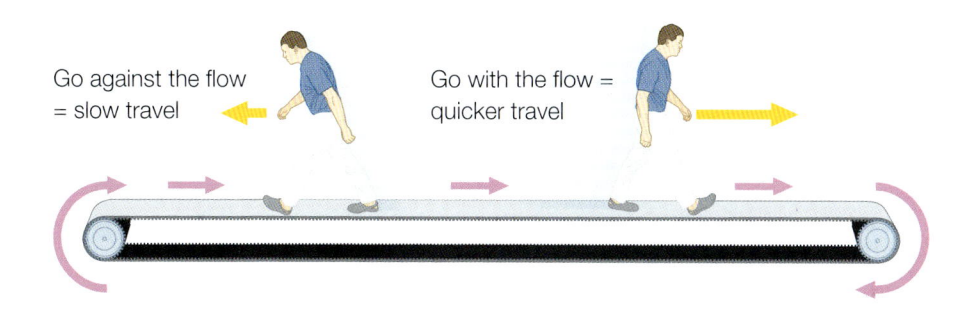

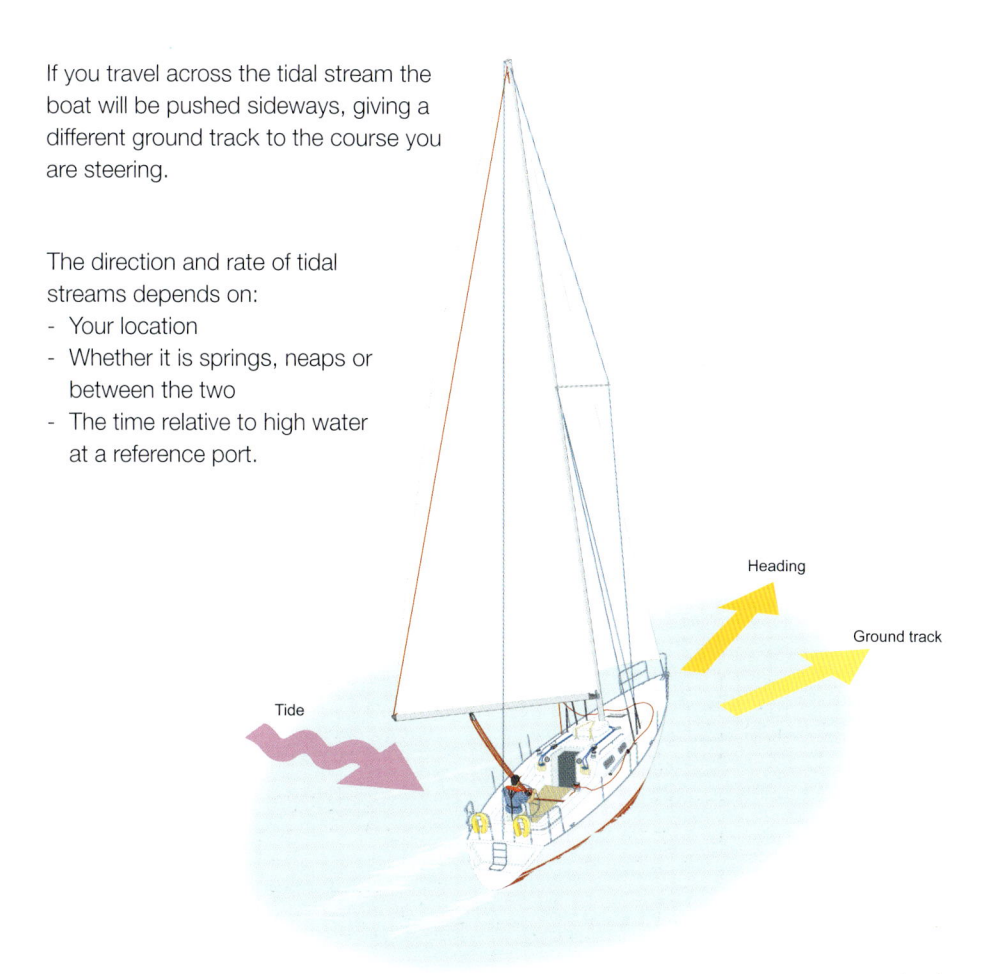

Go against the flow
= slow travel

Go with the flow =
quicker travel

If you travel across the tidal stream the boat will be pushed sideways, giving a different ground track to the course you are steering.

The direction and rate of tidal streams depends on:
- Your location
- Whether it is springs, neaps or between the two
- The time relative to high water at a reference port.

Heading

Ground track

Tide

## FINDING THE DIRECTION AND RATE OF THE TIDE

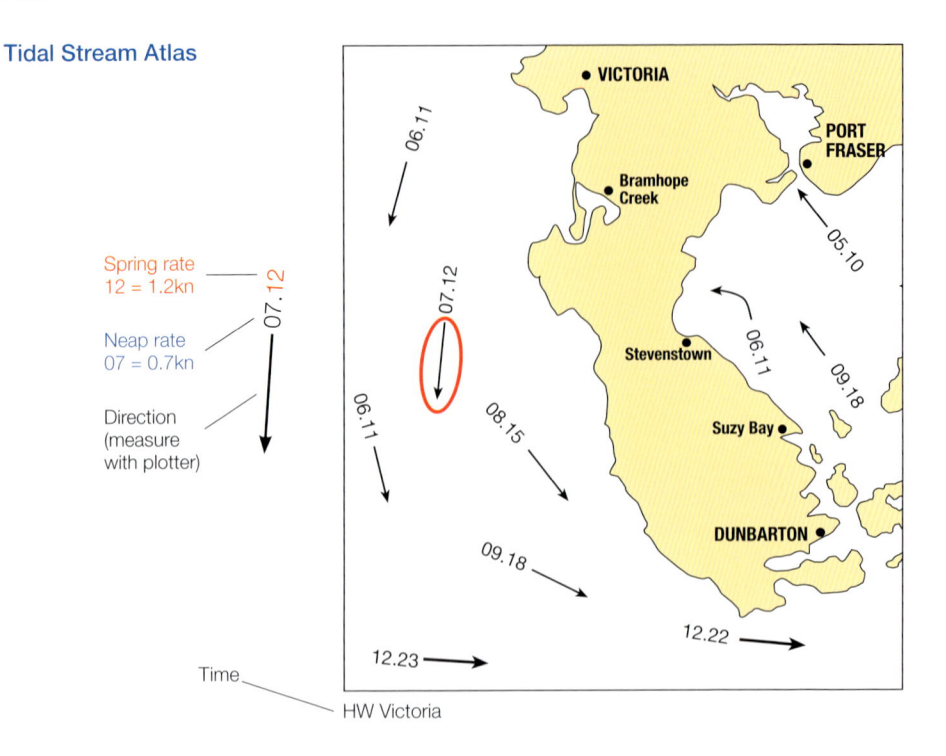

### Tidal Stream Atlas

Spring rate
12 = 1.2kn

Neap rate
07 = 0.7kn

Direction
(measure
with plotter)

Time

HW Victoria

### Tidal Diamond from Chart

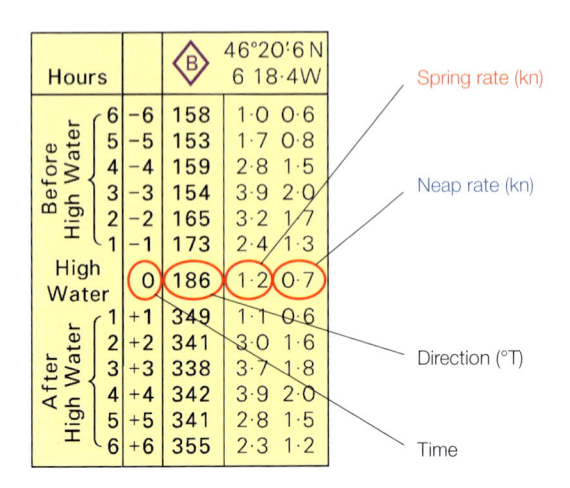

Victoria ⬦B⬦

| Hours | | B 46°20'.6N 6 18.4W | | |
|---|---|---|---|---|
| Before High Water | 6 -6 | 158 | 1.0 | 0.6 |
| | 5 -5 | 153 | 1.7 | 0.8 |
| | 4 -4 | 159 | 2.8 | 1.5 |
| | 3 -3 | 154 | 3.9 | 2.0 |
| | 2 -2 | 165 | 3.2 | 1.7 |
| | 1 -1 | 173 | 2.4 | 1.3 |
| High Water | 0 | 186 | 1.2 | 0.7 |
| After High Water | 1 +1 | 349 | 1.1 | 0.6 |
| | 2 +2 | 341 | 3.0 | 1.6 |
| | 3 +3 | 338 | 3.7 | 1.8 |
| | 4 +4 | 342 | 3.9 | 2.0 |
| | 5 +5 | 341 | 2.8 | 1.5 |
| | 6 +6 | 355 | 2.3 | 1.2 |

Spring rate (kn)

Neap rate (kn)

Direction (°T)

Time

[88]

Tidal Streams

### Example
What is the direction and rate of the tidal stream 5 miles south of Namley Harbour on Friday 24th May from 1045 to 1145?

**1** Find the time of HW and the heights of HW & LW at Victoria on Friday 24th May.

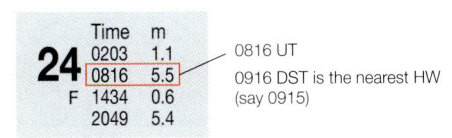

| | Time | m |
|---|---|---|
| **24** | 0203 | 1.1 |
| | 0816 | 5.5 |
| F | 1434 | 0.6 |
| | 2049 | 5.4 |

0816 UT
0916 DST is the nearest HW (say 0915)

**2** Is it springs, neaps or in between?

```
        5.5
      - 0.6
Range  4.9m   = Springs
```

| MEAN RANGES | |
|---|---|
| Springs | 4.9m |
| Neaps | 2.4m |

**3** How many hours before or after HW is 1045 to 1145?

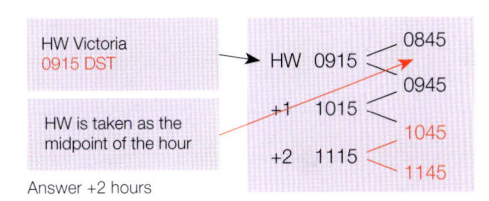

HW Victoria 0915 DST

HW is taken as the midpoint of the hour

Answer +2 hours

```
         0845
HW 0915
         0945
+1  1015
         1045
+2  1115
         1145
```

**4** Find the nearest ◇ to your position = Ⓐ

Spring rate = 1.6kn
Direction of tidal stream = 111°(T)

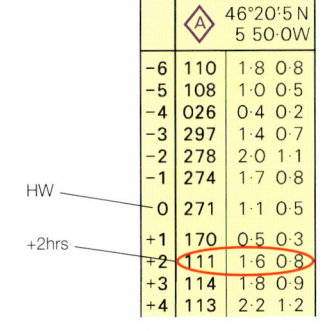

| | Ⓐ 46°20′5 N 5 50·0 W | |
|---|---|---|
| -6 | 110 | 1·8 0·8 |
| -5 | 108 | 1·0 0·5 |
| -4 | 026 | 0·4 0·2 |
| -3 | 297 | 1·4 0·7 |
| -2 | 278 | 2·0 1·1 |
| -1 | 274 | 1·7 0·8 |
| HW 0 | 271 | 1·1 0·5 |
| +1 | 170 | 0·5 0·3 |
| +2hrs  +2 | 111 | 1·6 0·8 |
| +3 | 114 | 1·8 0·9 |
| +4 | 113 | 2·2 1·2 |

**5** Or using a tidal stream atlas, which is the nearest arrow?

Measure direction of arrow 111°(T) Spring rate 1.6kn

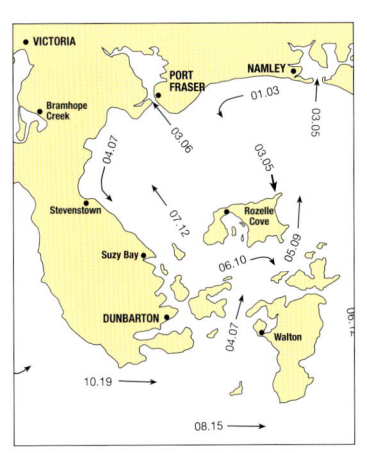

HW Victoria +1   1015 (0945–1045) 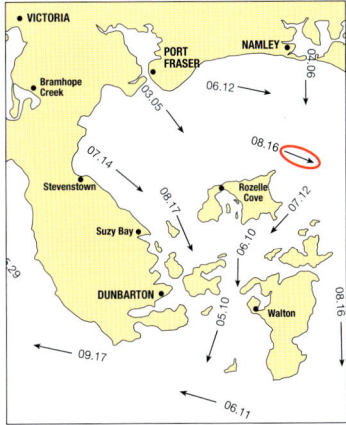                HW Victoria +2   1115 (1045–1145)

[ 89 ]

Dead Reckoning Position

# Dead Reckoning Position

It's possible to reckon your approximate position if you know a) the course steered, and b) the distance travelled (measured on a log).

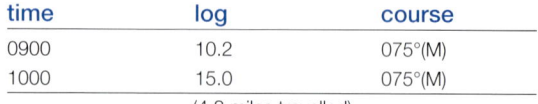

| time | log | course |
|------|------|--------|
| 0900 | 10.2 | 075°(M) |
| 1000 | 15.0 | 075°(M) |

(4.8 miles travelled)

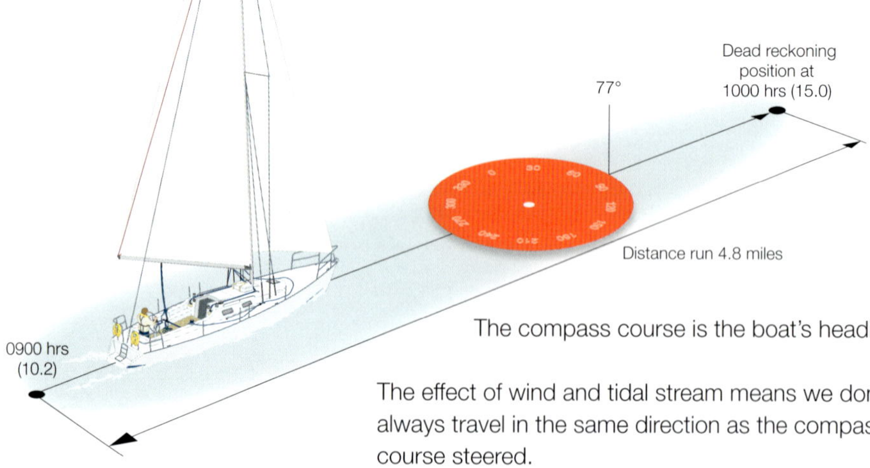

Dead reckoning position at 1000 hrs (15.0)

77°

Distance run 4.8 miles

0900 hrs (10.2)

The compass course is the boat's heading.

The effect of wind and tidal stream means we don't always travel in the same direction as the compass course steered.

## Effect of Leeway

Actual course 070°(M)
005° leeway
WIND
Heading 075°(M)

## Effect of Tidal Stream

The boat is taken by the direction and rate of the tidal stream.

TIDAL STREAM

# Estimated Position

## To Plot an EP

| time | log | course | leeway | wind | tidal stream |
|------|------|---------|--------|------|--------------|
| 0900 | 10.2 | 075°(M) | 5° | N5 | |
| 1000 | 15.0 | 075°(M) | 5° | N5 | 120°(T) 2.0kn for 0900–1000 |

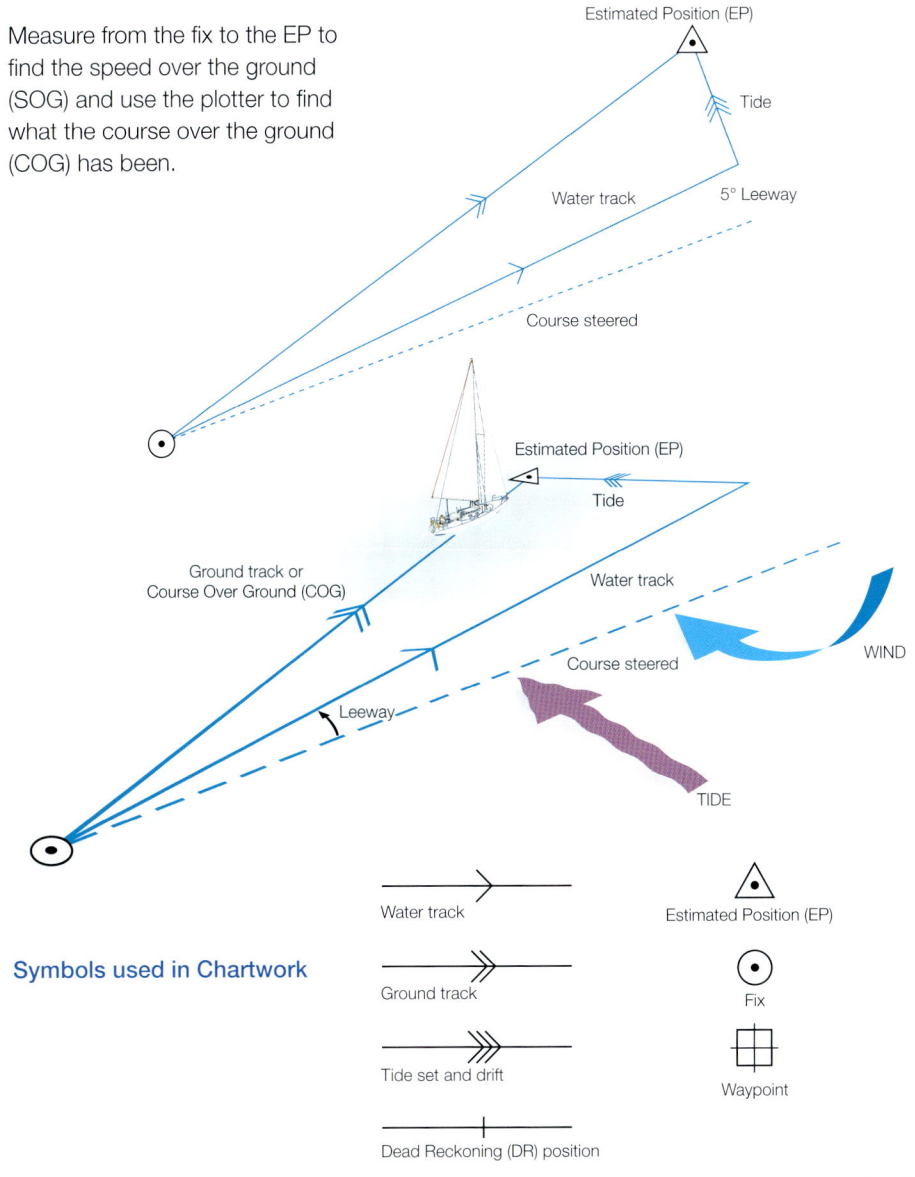

Measure from the fix to the EP to find the speed over the ground (SOG) and use the plotter to find what the course over the ground (COG) has been.

## Symbols used in Chartwork

- Water track
- Ground track
- Tide set and drift
- Dead Reckoning (DR) position
- Estimated Position (EP)
- Fix
- Waypoint

Course to Steer

# Course to Steer

A person rowing across a river instinctively angles the boat upstream to counter the effect of the current.

At sea we often can't see our destination so we need to calculate how much to angle into the tidal stream to make the most direct passage.

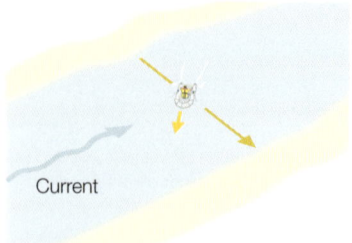

Current

For example:
What is the course to steer from position A to waypoint B at 1045 DST on Friday 24 May?

**1** How far is it from A to B?
Answer: 8.5 miles.

**2** Approximately how long will it take to travel 8.5 miles if my speed is 9 knots?
Answer: Roughly an hour.

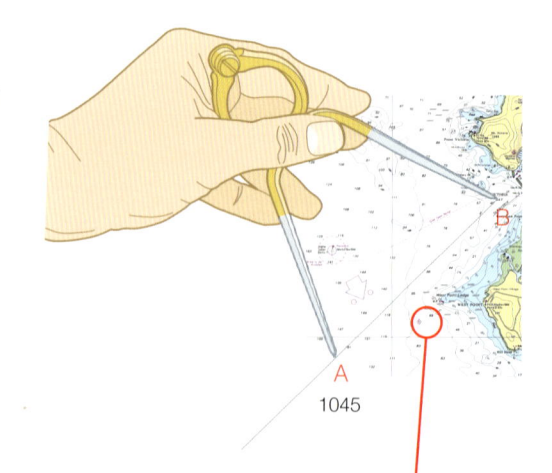

A
1045

**3** Leaving position A at 1045, how will the tidal stream affect my passage for the next hour?

- Using RYA Training Chart 3, find the tidal stream reference port (Victoria).

- Find the time of HW and establish springs or neaps. Friday 24 May HW Victoria = 0916 DST range 4.9 (springs).

- Use the closest tidal diamond ⬨B⬨ to establish rate and direction. You could also use a tidal atlas.

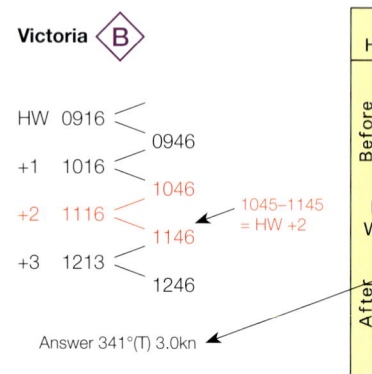

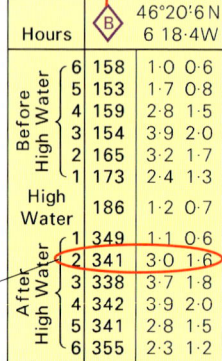

Victoria ⬨B⬨

HW 0916
             0946
+1  1016
             1046
+2  1116                1045–1145
             1146       = HW +2
+3  1213
             1246

Answer 341°(T) 3.0kn

| Hours | | ⬨B⬨ 46°20·6 N 6 18·4 W |  |
|---|---|---|---|
| Before High Water | 6 | 158 | 1·0 0·6 |
| | 5 | 153 | 1·7 0·8 |
| | 4 | 159 | 2·8 1·5 |
| | 3 | 154 | 3·9 2·0 |
| | 2 | 165 | 3·2 1·7 |
| | 1 | 173 | 2·4 1·3 |
| High Water | | 186 | 1·2 0·7 |
| After High Water | 1 | 349 | 1·1 0·6 |
| | 2 | 341 | 3·0 1·6 |
| | 3 | 338 | 3·7 1·8 |
| | 4 | 342 | 3·9 2·0 |
| | 5 | 341 | 2·8 1·5 |
| | 6 | 355 | 2·3 1·2 |

Course to Steer

**4** Plot the tidal stream at the start of the ground track.

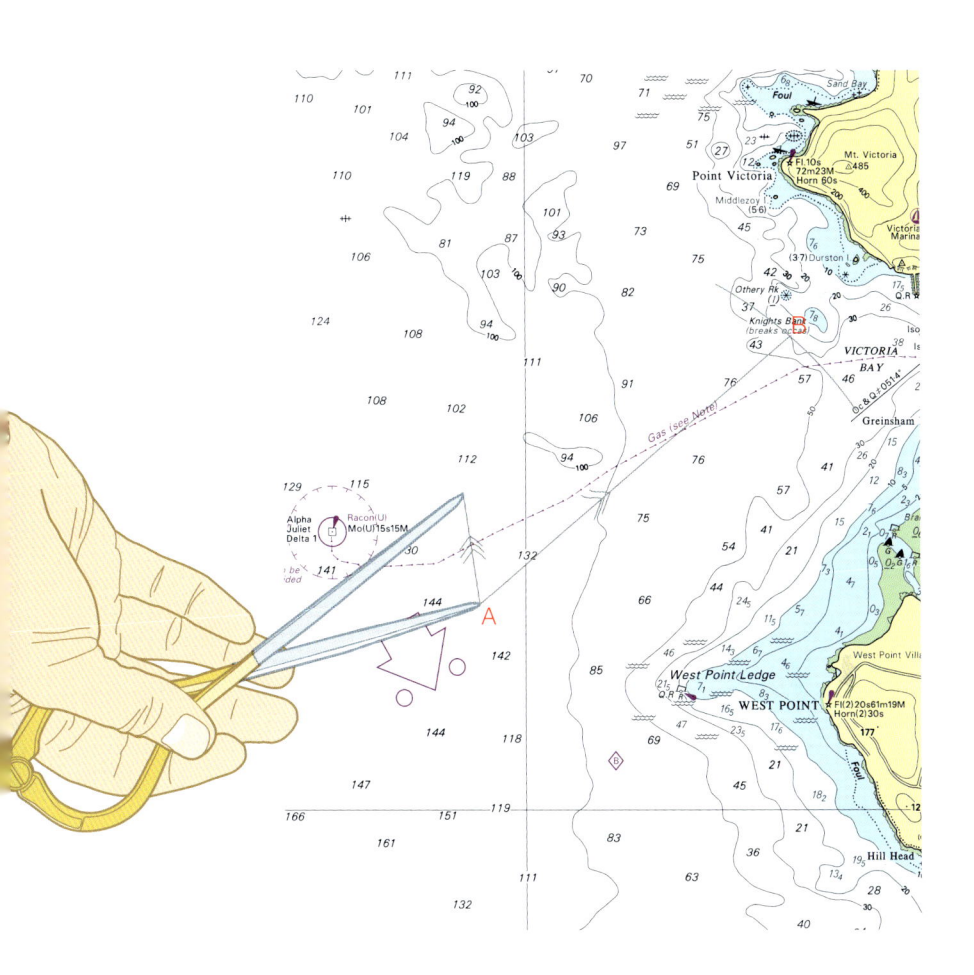

[ 93 ]

Course to Steer

**5** Measure the expected boat speed for one hour (9kn) and arc dividers from end of tidal stream to cross the ground track. This usually goes beyond or falls short of B.

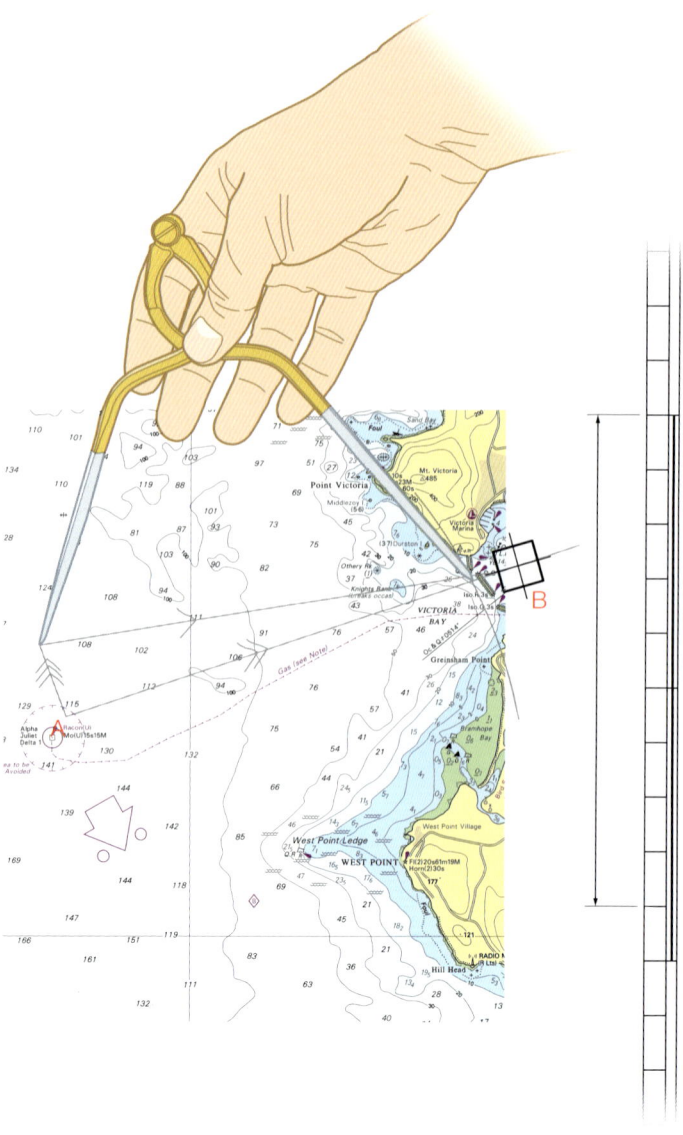

Course to Steer

**6** Measure direction of water track. This will be your course to steer.

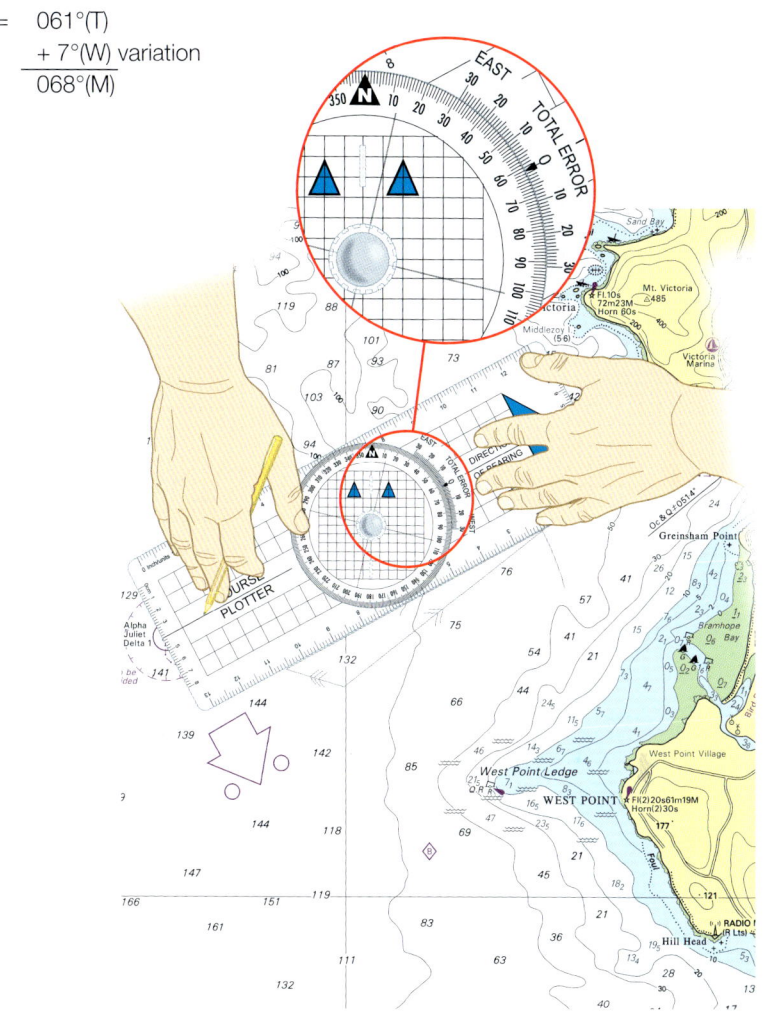

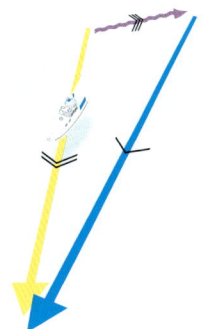

= 061°(T)
  + 7°(W) variation
  ‾‾‾‾‾‾‾‾‾‾‾‾‾‾‾
  068°(M)

Although you are steering 068 degrees (M), you are maintaining your shortest COG or ground track (051 degrees (M)) A to B.

7. Consider leeway. Head up 5 degrees or 10 degrees into the wind if necessary.

Fixing your Position

# Fixing your Position

## A VISUAL FIX

### Three-Point Fix

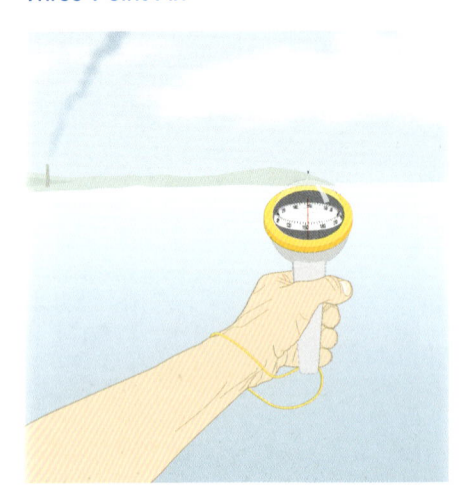

Take bearings on charted objects to fix your position.

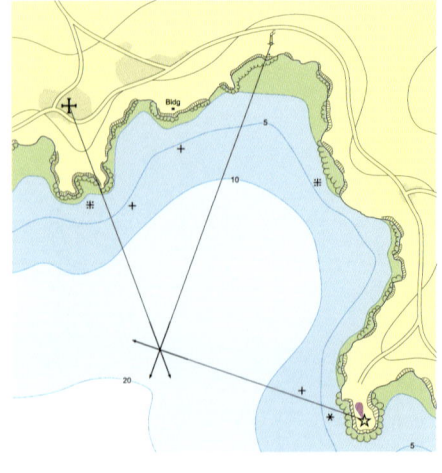

Draw the bearings on the chart. Your position will be where the lines intersect. Use closer objects for greater accuracy.

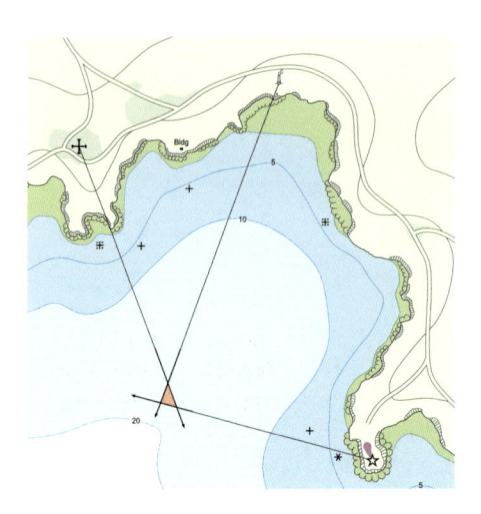

Bearings rarely line up as a perfect fix. Error produces a cocked hat.

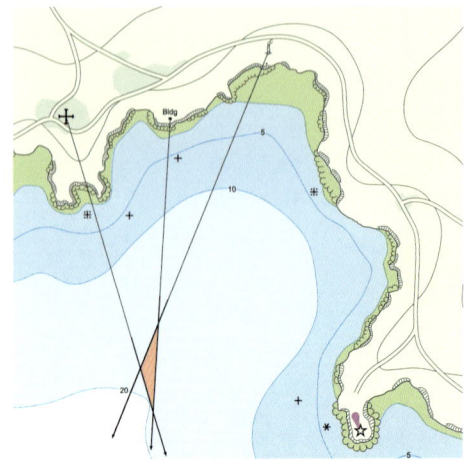

If bearings are too close together the error is greater. Don't use objects that will give a poor angle of cut.

Fixing your Position

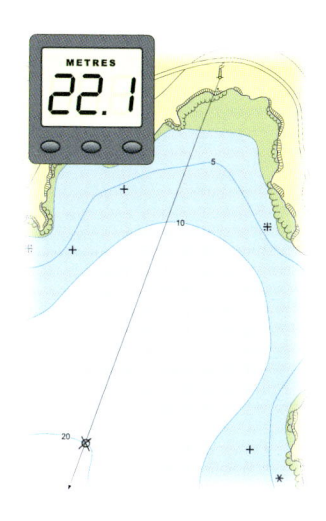

### Bearing and Contour
Fix your position by taking a bearing on a charted object. Don't forget to allow for the height of tide.

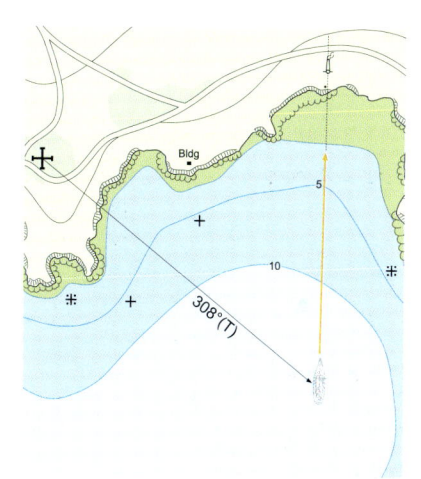

### Transit and Bearing
Line up two charted objects to make a transit. This gives you a very accurate position line.

Chimney and flag staff

### The Simplest Fix
Plot your position as you pass a charted object.

Fixing your Position

## A GPS FIX

A GPS receiver obtains a fix from signals transmitted by orbiting satellites. This gives a position which is accurate to about 15 metres.

GPS is generally reliable and accurate but, as with all electronics, it can go wrong. The main things that can affect it are power or aerial failure; transmissions from mobile phones; interruptions or changes to the satellite system.

The simplest way to use GPS is to plot your position from the longitude and latitude given on the display.

It can also give your current course and speed over the ground, and information about your position in relation to waypoints.

Fixing your Position

**Always Back-up your GPS Position with Information from another Source such as:**

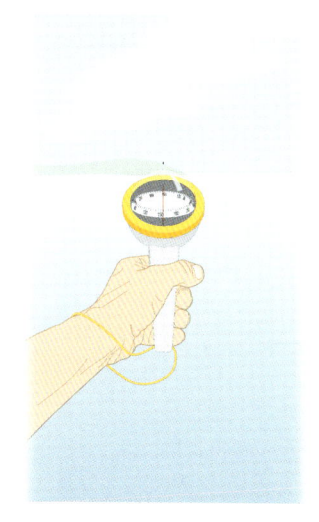

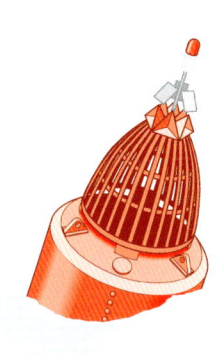

Bearing.

A charted object (IALA B buoyage).

Keep a record of your position at regular intervals on the chart and in the ship's log.

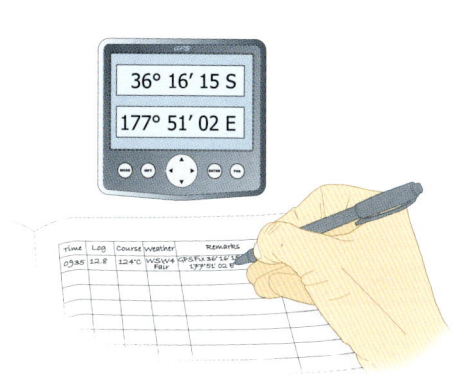

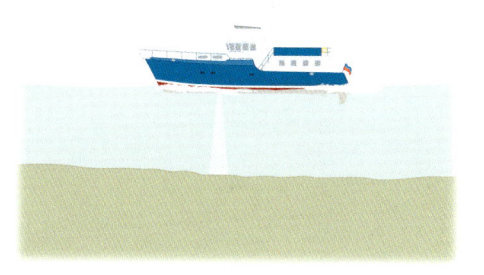

Depth allowing for tide.

[ 99 ]

# Waypoints

Waypoints (WPTs) are tools to help you navigate. They are positions stored in the memory of a GPS and used as reference points.

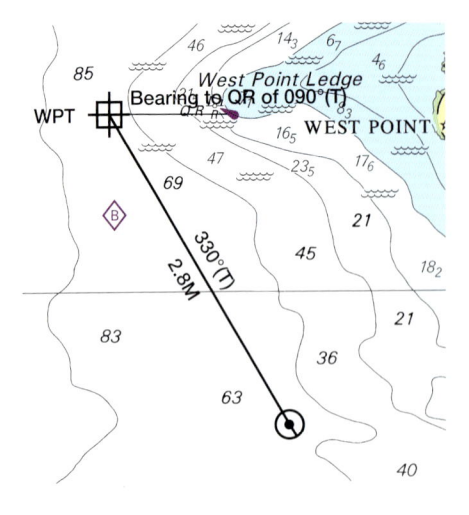

For example, you could use a WPT placed at the entrance of a harbour to help guide you safely into port or as part of a route.

You obtain WPTs from:
- the chart. Select the position and measure the latitude and longitude.
- publications such as almanacs, directories and magazines. Check before use.

The GPS display can show the direction and distance to a waypoint and your COG and SOG.

Be careful when you input a waypoint into a GPS. Always check that the direction and distance given by the GPS matches that measured on the chart. Any difference means that you have probably entered the WPT latitude and longitude incorrectly.

Never input a waypoint straight from a book or magazine. Always plot it on a chart to check your route.

Plot your waypoint adjacent to rather than directly on charted objects. You could hit them!

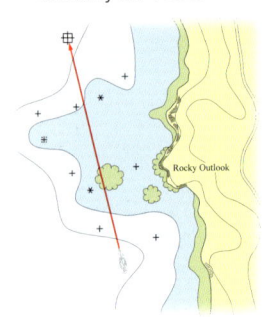

In busy areas, bear in mind that lots of boats could be using the same waypoint.

Where possible, plot your waypoint in a position that can be confirmed by visual references or depth.

# Waypoints

## OTHER WAYS OF USING WAYPOINTS

You can plot your position quickly and simply by entering easily found positions as waypoints. The GPS will give you a direction and distance to the waypoint and you can plot these to give a fix. This is easier, quicker and less prone to error than plotting latitude and longitude, but double check that you have entered the waypoint correctly.

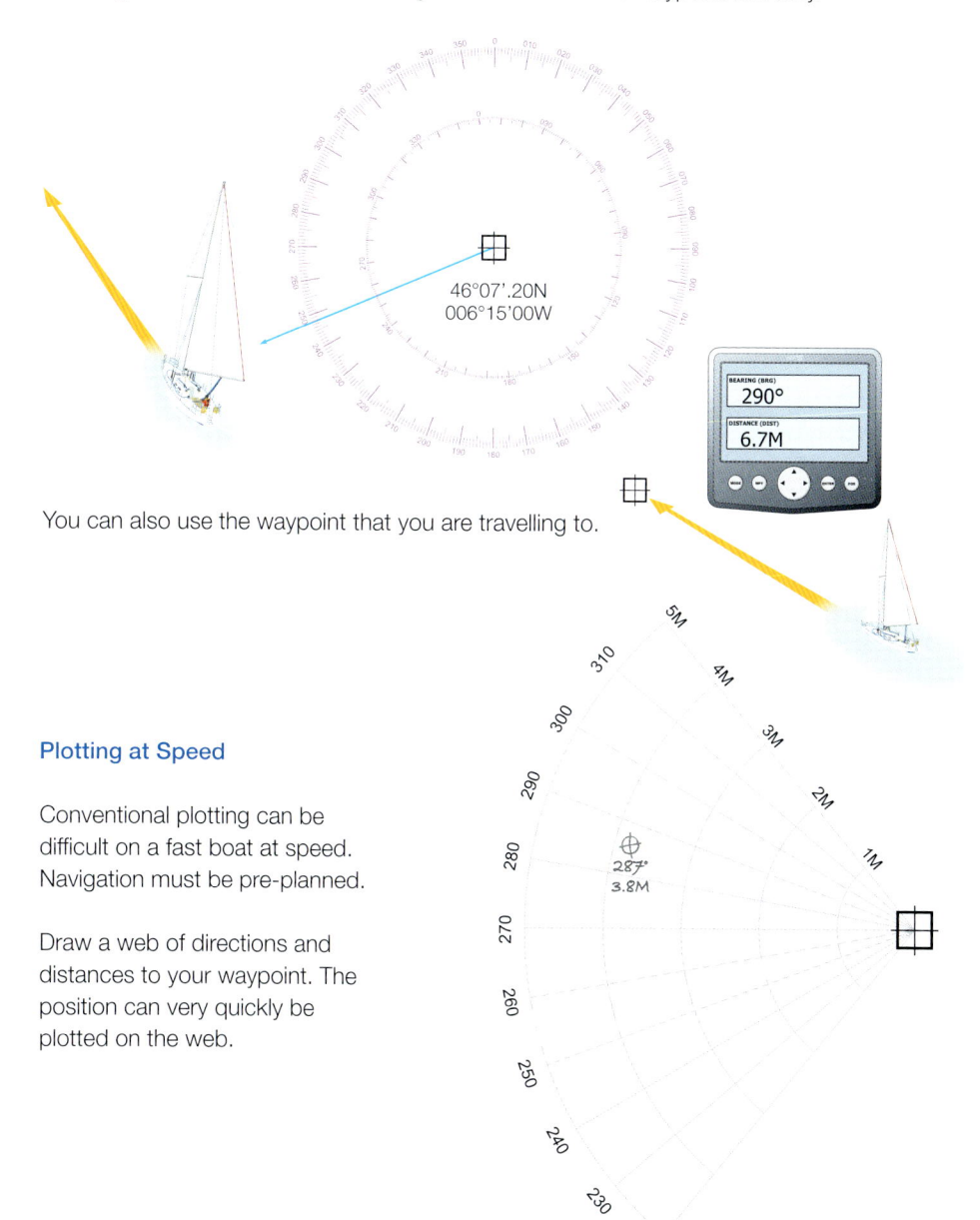

46°07'.20N
006°15'00W

BEARING (BRG)
290°

DISTANCE (DIST)
6.7M

You can also use the waypoint that you are travelling to.

## Plotting at Speed

Conventional plotting can be difficult on a fast boat at speed. Navigation must be pre-planned.

Draw a web of directions and distances to your waypoint. The position can very quickly be plotted on the web.

287°
3.8M

[ 101 ]

Waypoints

## Be Careful

Remember that GPS doesn't allow for tidal stream.

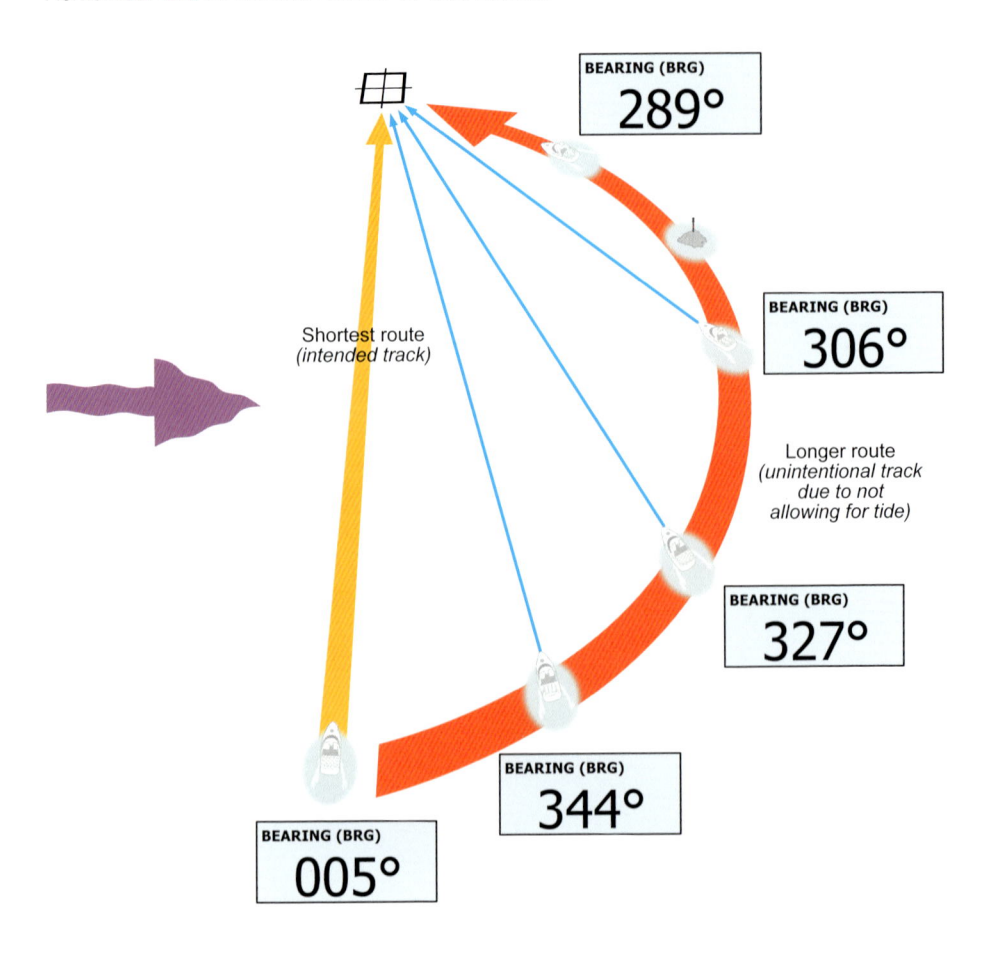

**BEARING (BRG)** **289°**

**BEARING (BRG)** **306°**

Shortest route
*(intended track)*

Longer route
*(unintentional track due to not allowing for tide)*

**BEARING (BRG)** **327°**

**BEARING (BRG)** **344°**

**BEARING (BRG)** **005°**

It seems easy just to steer the direction to a waypoint that the GPS gives, but if there is significant crosstide you will sail a longer route and could put the boat in danger.

Always pre-plan a course to steer to allow for tidal stream. It's more efficient.

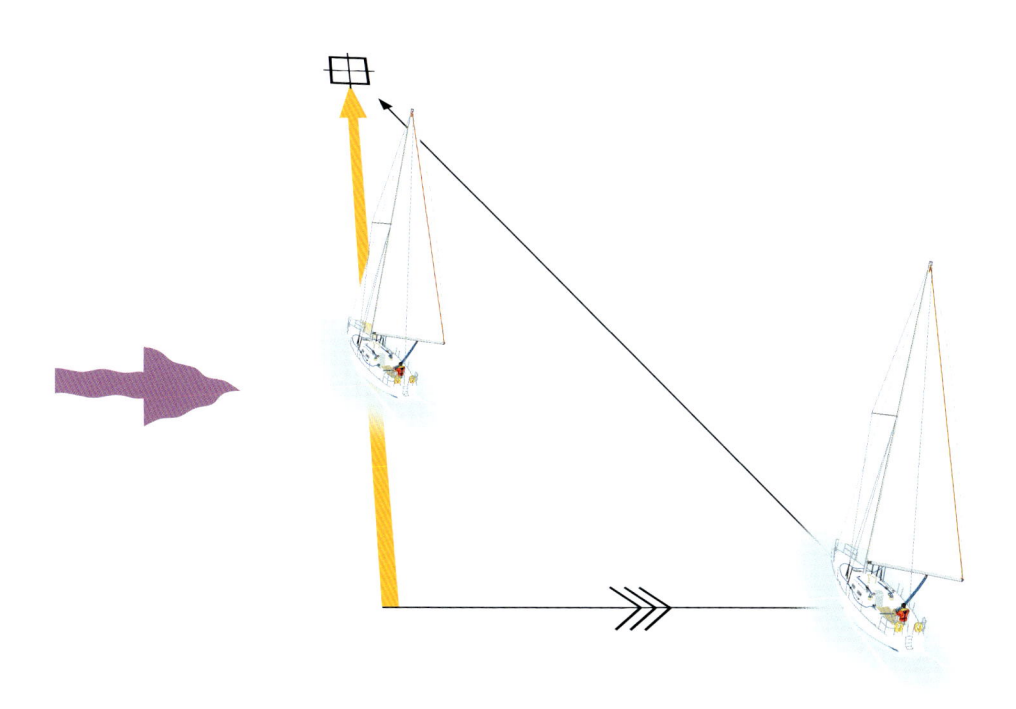

# Buoyage

## IALA – MARITIME BUOYAGE SYSTEM

Two buoyage systems, IALA A and IALA B, exist in the world. The difference affects the colour and light characteristics of lateral marks. IALA A is used in Europe, Africa, Russia, India, Australia and New Zealand. IALA B is used in the USA, South America, parts of the Caribbean, South-East Asia and Canada.

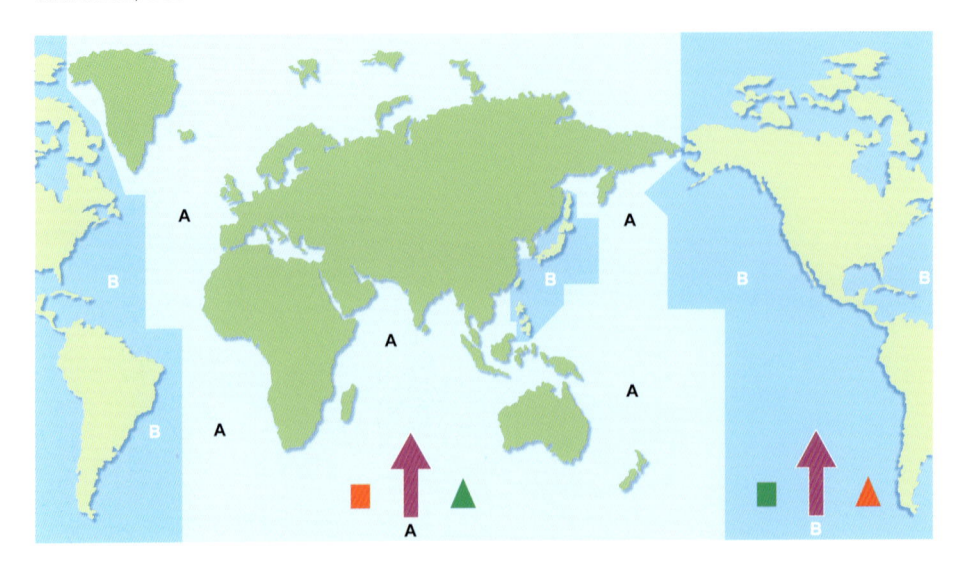

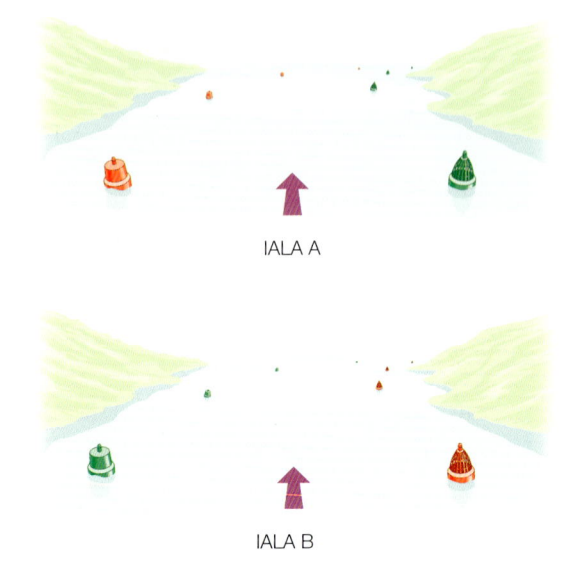

IALA A

IALA B

Buoyage

## IALA A BUOYAGE

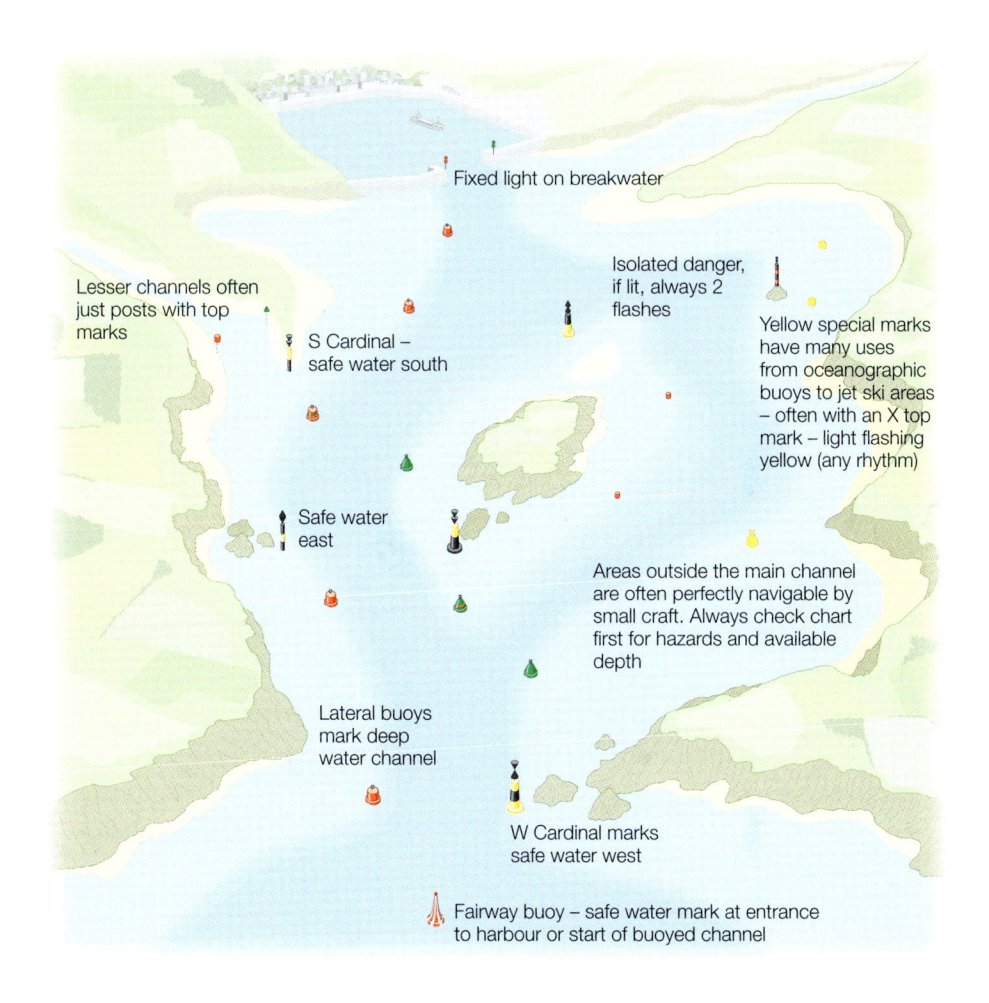

Fixed light on breakwater

Lesser channels often just posts with top marks

S Cardinal – safe water south

Isolated danger, if lit, always 2 flashes

Yellow special marks have many uses from oceanographic buoys to jet ski areas – often with an X top mark – light flashing yellow (any rhythm)

Safe water east

Areas outside the main channel are often perfectly navigable by small craft. Always check chart first for hazards and available depth

Lateral buoys mark deep water channel

W Cardinal marks safe water west

Fairway buoy – safe water mark at entrance to harbour or start of buoyed channel

### Lateral Marks

Used to mark channels. Leave starboard cone to your starboard side when going into harbour.

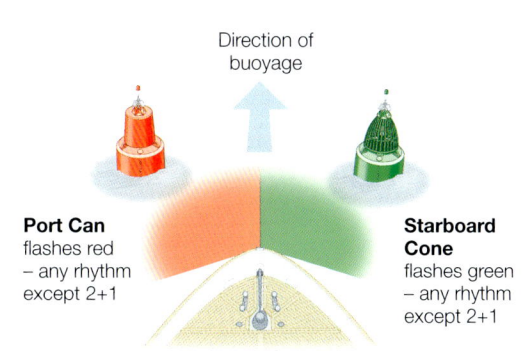

Direction of buoyage

**Port Can**
flashes red
– any rhythm
except 2+1

**Starboard Cone**
flashes green
– any rhythm
except 2+1

[ 105 ]

## Buoyage

## IALA B BUOYAGE

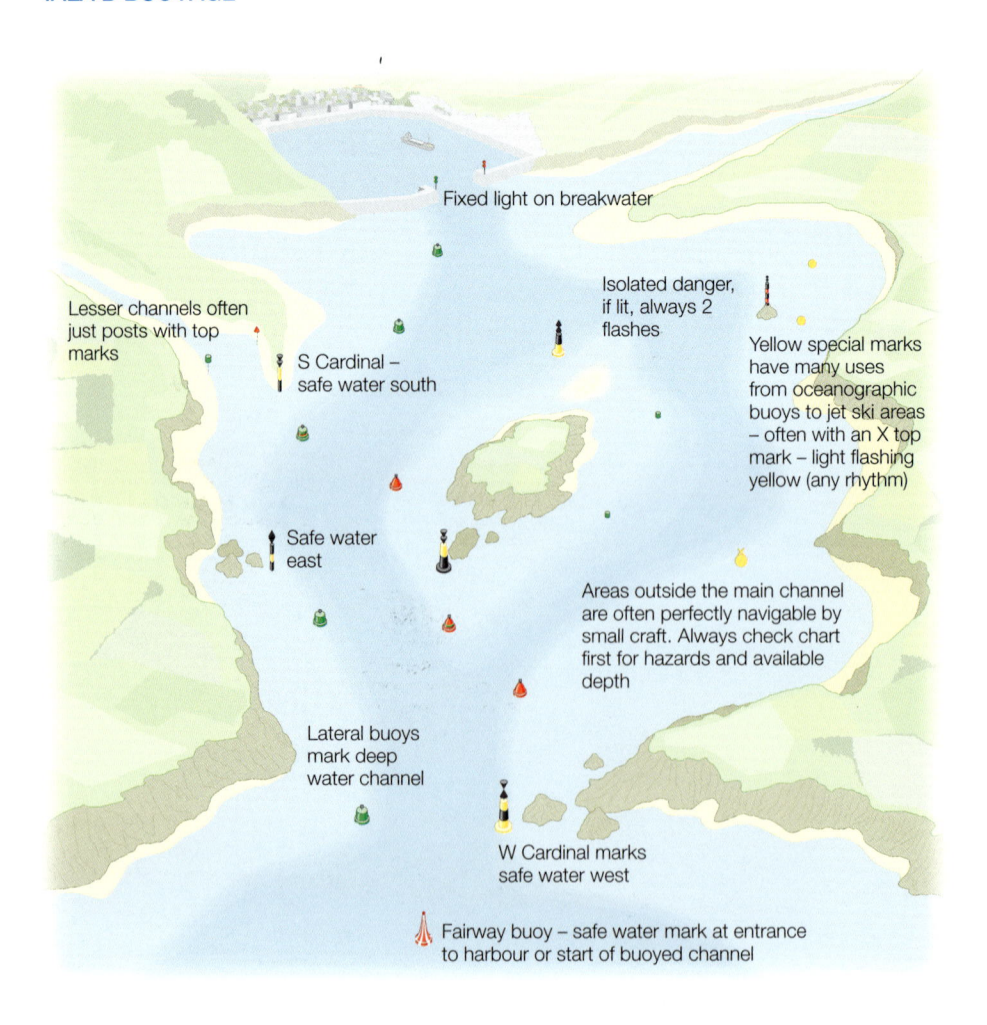

Fixed light on breakwater

Lesser channels often just posts with top marks

S Cardinal – safe water south

Isolated danger, if lit, always 2 flashes

Yellow special marks have many uses from oceanographic buoys to jet ski areas – often with an X top mark – light flashing yellow (any rhythm)

Safe water east

Areas outside the main channel are often perfectly navigable by small craft. Always check chart first for hazards and available depth

Lateral buoys mark deep water channel

W Cardinal marks safe water west

Fairway buoy – safe water mark at entrance to harbour or start of buoyed channel

### Lateral Marks

Used to mark channels. Leave starboard cone to your starboard side when going into harbour.

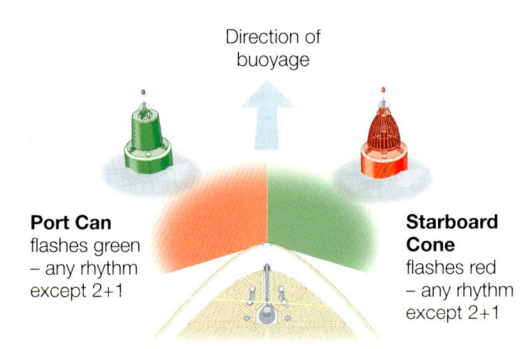

Direction of buoyage

**Port Can**
flashes green
– any rhythm
except 2+1

**Starboard Cone**
flashes red
– any rhythm
except 2+1

[ 106 ]

Buoyage

## CARDINAL MARKS

### Cardinals

Cardinal marks indicate which side of the mark is safe water and remain constant throughout the IALA system. Cones point to black bands. Buoys are found in many shapes and sizes. Solar panels and lights can make top marks difficult to distinguish.
Weeds and guano can alter the appearance and colour.

**North Cardinal**
Colour: Black/yellow (BY on charts)
Shapes: Both pointing upwards to north

**West Cardinal**
Colour: Yellow/black/yellow (YBY on charts)
Shapes: Top facing downwards, bottom upwards forming a bobbin shape

**East Cardinal**
Colour: Black/yellow/black (BYB on charts)
Shapes: Top pointing upwards, bottom downwards forming a diamond shape

**South Cardinal**
Colour: Yellow/black (YB on charts)
Shapes: Both pointing downwards to south

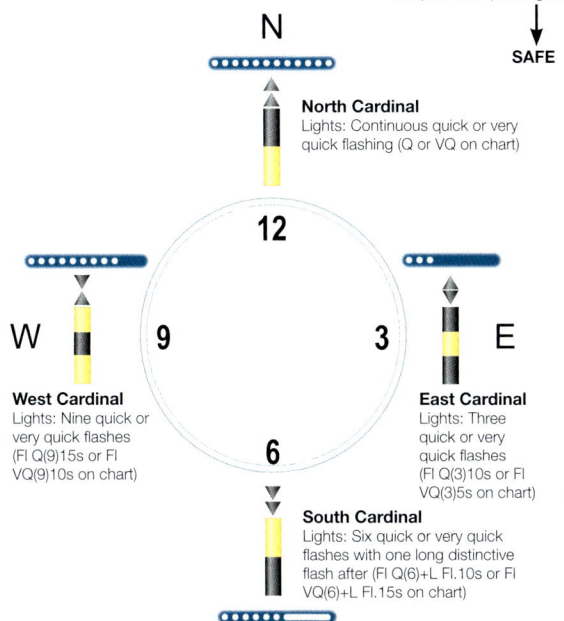

**North Cardinal**
Lights: Continuous quick or very quick flashing (Q or VQ on chart)

**West Cardinal**
Lights: Nine quick or very quick flashes (Fl Q(9)15s or Fl VQ(9)10s on chart)

**East Cardinal**
Lights: Three quick or very quick flashes (Fl Q(3)10s or Fl VQ(3)5s on chart)

**South Cardinal**
Lights: Six quick or very quick flashes with one long distinctive flash after (Fl Q(6)+L Fl.10s or Fl VQ(6)+L Fl.15s on chart)

Buoyage

## Emergency Wreck-marking Buoy

Emergency wreck-marking buoy, placed at the site of a new wreck. Remains in place until the wreck has been dealt with.

## Preferred Channel Marks IALA A

Preferred channel mark, may be placed where a channel splits in two, indicating the preferred channel.

# Lights

## SECTOR LIGHTS

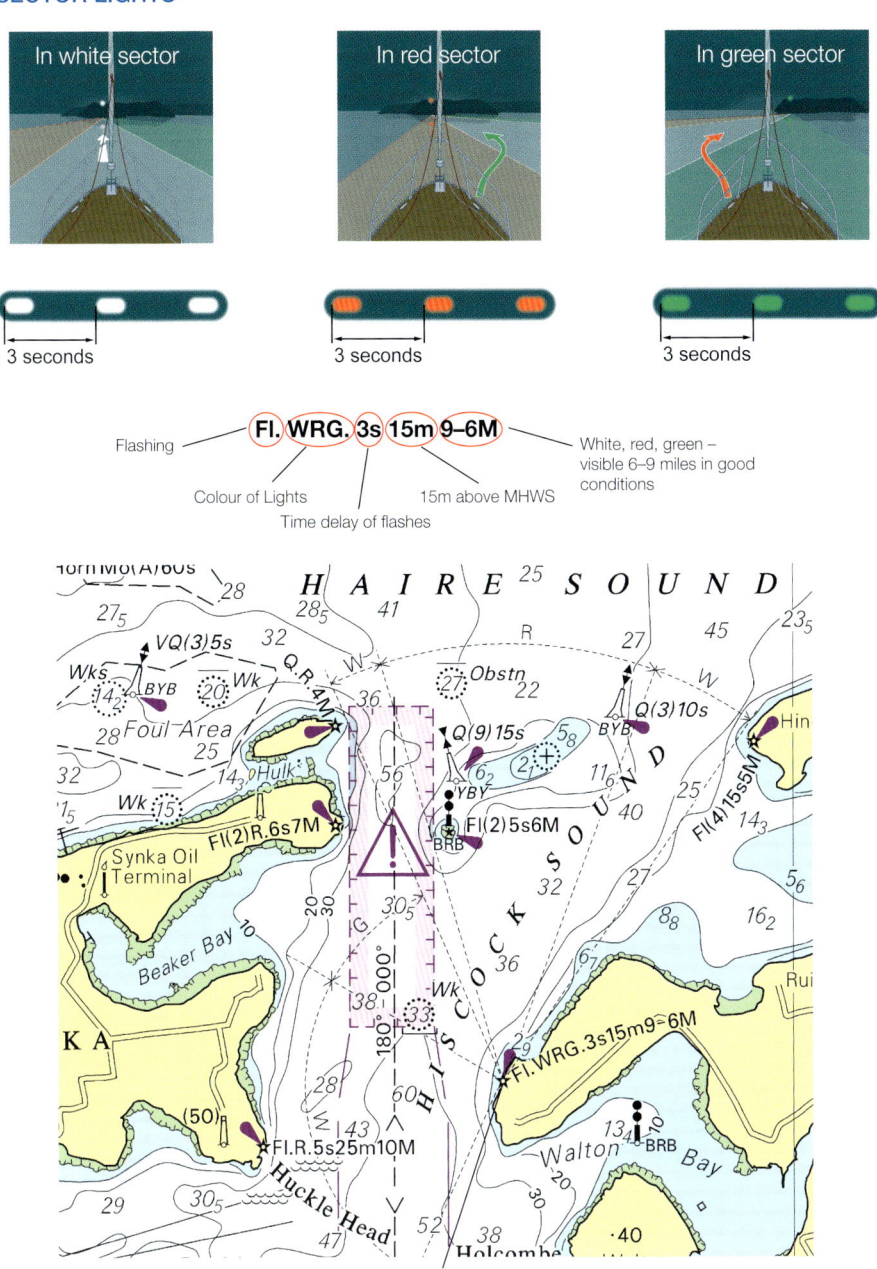

In white sector

In red sector

In green sector

3 seconds

3 seconds

3 seconds

Flashing — **Fl. WRG. 3s 15m 9–6M** — White, red, green – visible 6–9 miles in good conditions

Colour of Lights

15m above MHWS

Time delay of flashes

e.g. Evans Head Lighthouse

Lights

## LEADING LIGHTS

Leading lights guide you in and out of harbour.

Too far to starboard.                On course.                Too far to port.

## LIGHTHOUSES

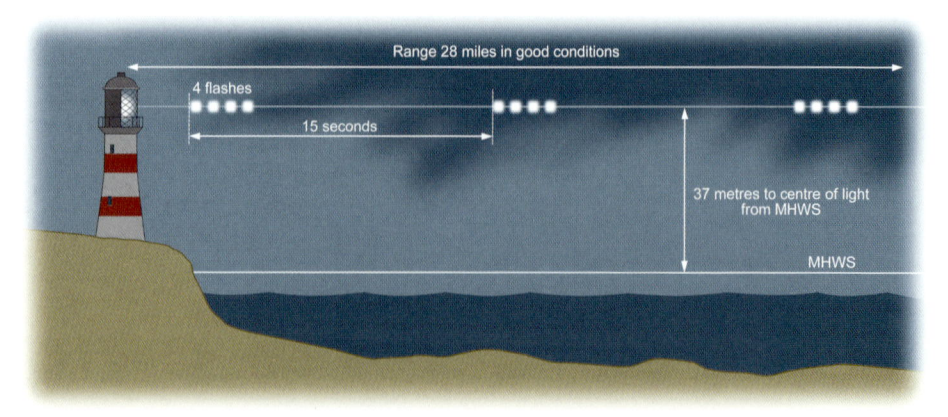

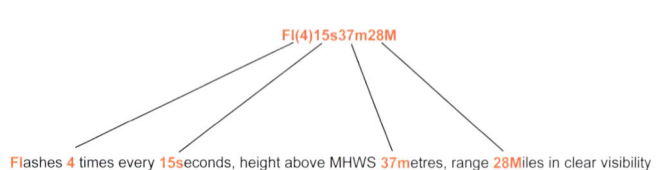

Range 28 miles in good conditions
4 flashes
15 seconds
37 metres to centre of light from MHWS
MHWS

Fl(4)15s37m28M

Flashes 4 times every 15seconds, height above MHWS 37metres, range 28Miles in clear visibility

## Other Light Characteristics

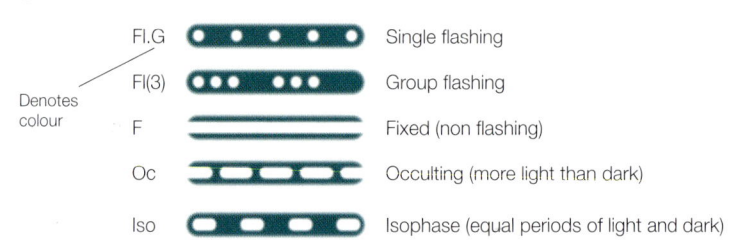

Denotes colour

Fl.G — Single flashing
Fl(3) — Group flashing
F — Fixed (non flashing)
Oc — Occulting (more light than dark)
Iso — Isophase (equal periods of light and dark)

# Pilotage

Pilotage is the art of inshore navigation when you have visual references to help you find your way along the coast and in and out of harbour. There may be lots of different hazards so good planning is essential.
Don't spend too much time down below – you will soon lose track of where you are and put yourself in danger. Making a good plan means you can navigate from on deck.

## THINGS YOU MIGHT NEED TO PLAN FOR

Rocks.

Shoals and shallows.

Shipping channels.

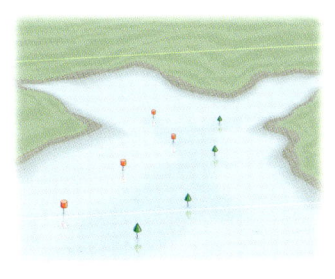

How an expanse of water changes at high water...

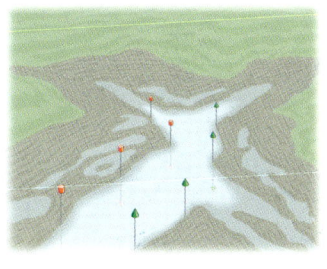

... and at low water.

Chain ferries.

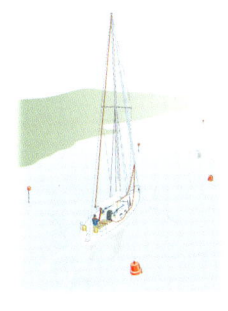

Harbour byelaws e.g. small craft channels.

Speed restriction in channel.

Effect of tide.

A different port may have a change of buoyage system. Here, it is IALA A buoyage.

[ 111 ]

Pilotage

## TECHNIQUES

### Transits

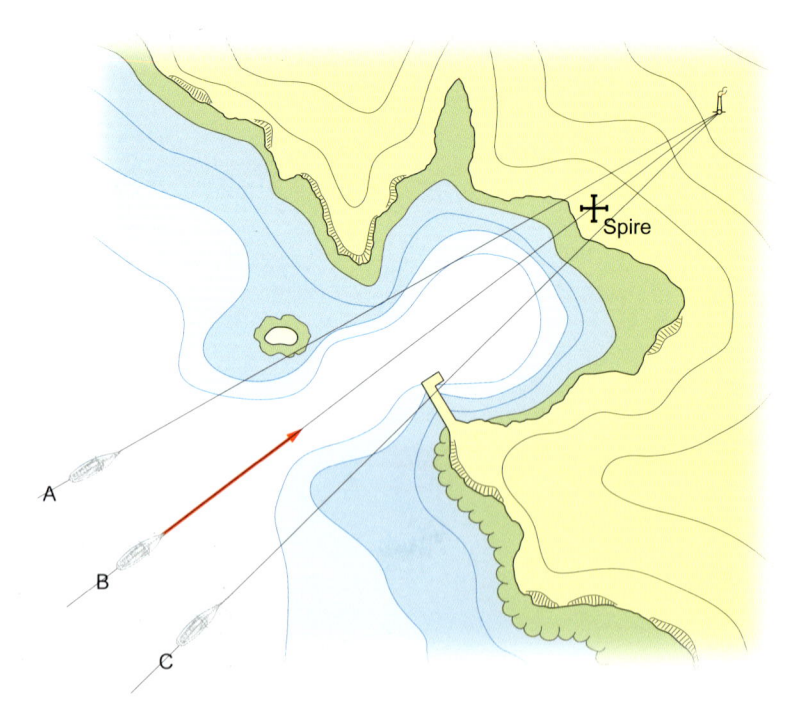

A = Too far to port

B = On track

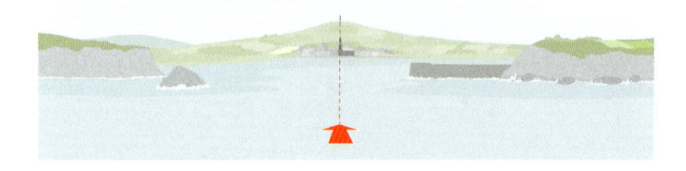

C = Too far to starboard

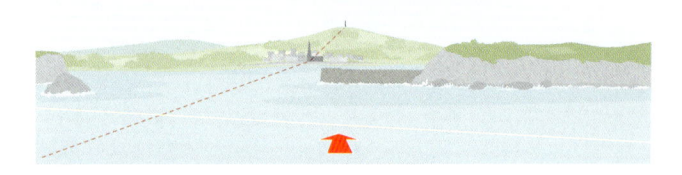

[ 112 ]

Pilotage

## Contours

You can work out where you are when you cross a contour. They can be followed in poor visibility. Remember to allow for rise and fall of tide.

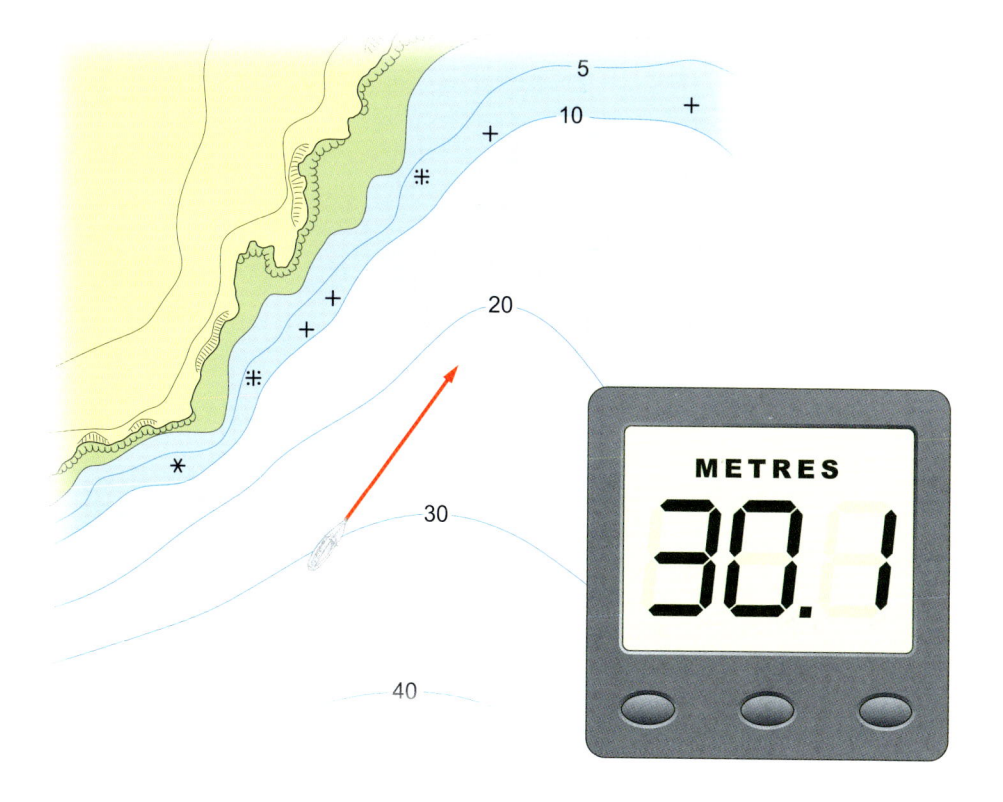

Pilotage

## Clearing Bearing

You can go anywhere between the two bearings.

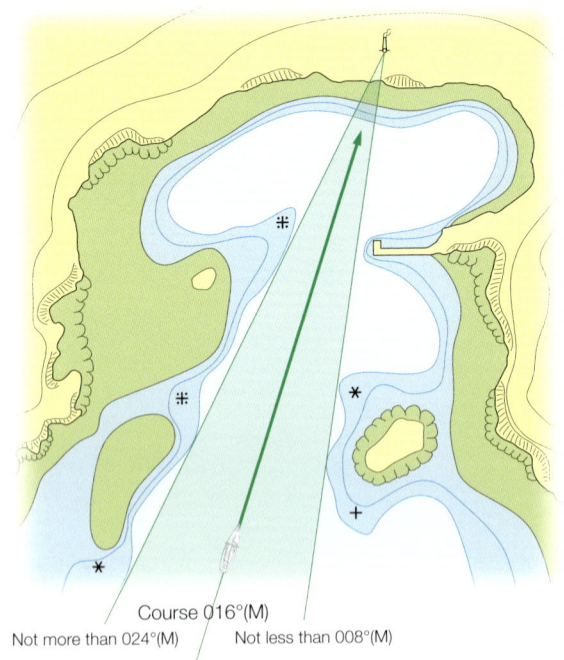

Course 016°(M)
Not more than 024°(M)   Not less than 008°(M)

## Back Bearing

Spire

Course 335°(M)± to keep back bearing 155°(M)

[ 114 ]

Pilotage

## Bearing & Distance

Work this out in advance so you know where to expect the next buoy.

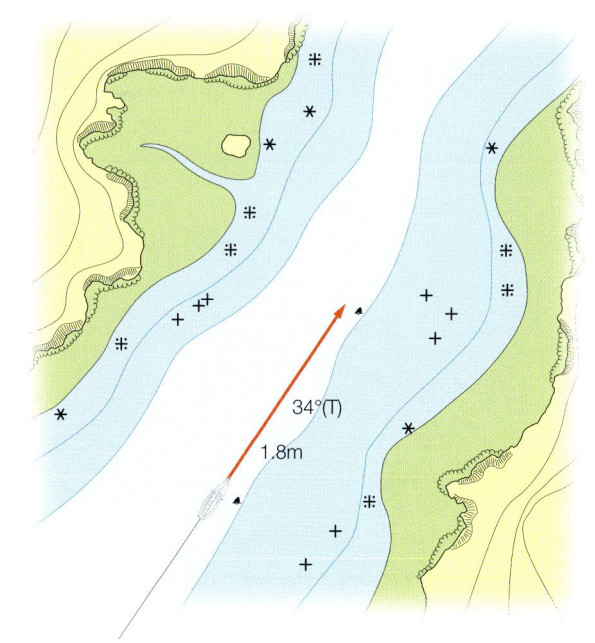

Course 34°(T). Distance between buoys 1.8 miles

## Turning Points

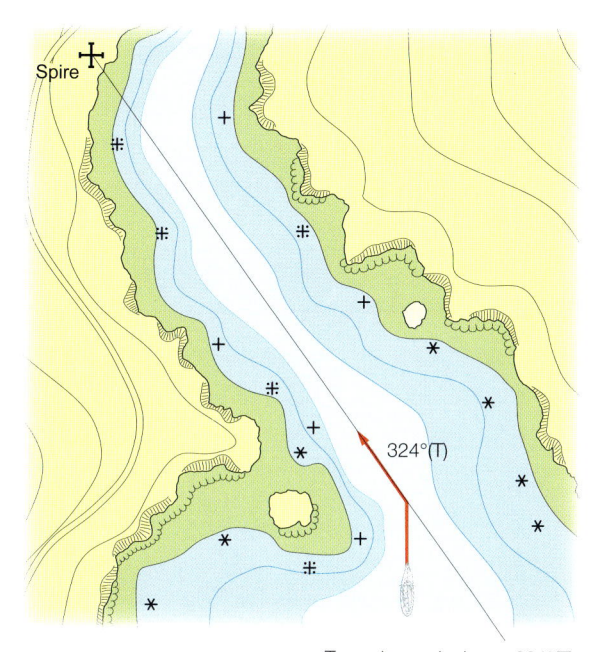

Turn when spire bears 324°(T)

[ 115 ]

# Making and Following a Pilotage Plan

Making and Following a Pilotage Plan

# Following your Plan

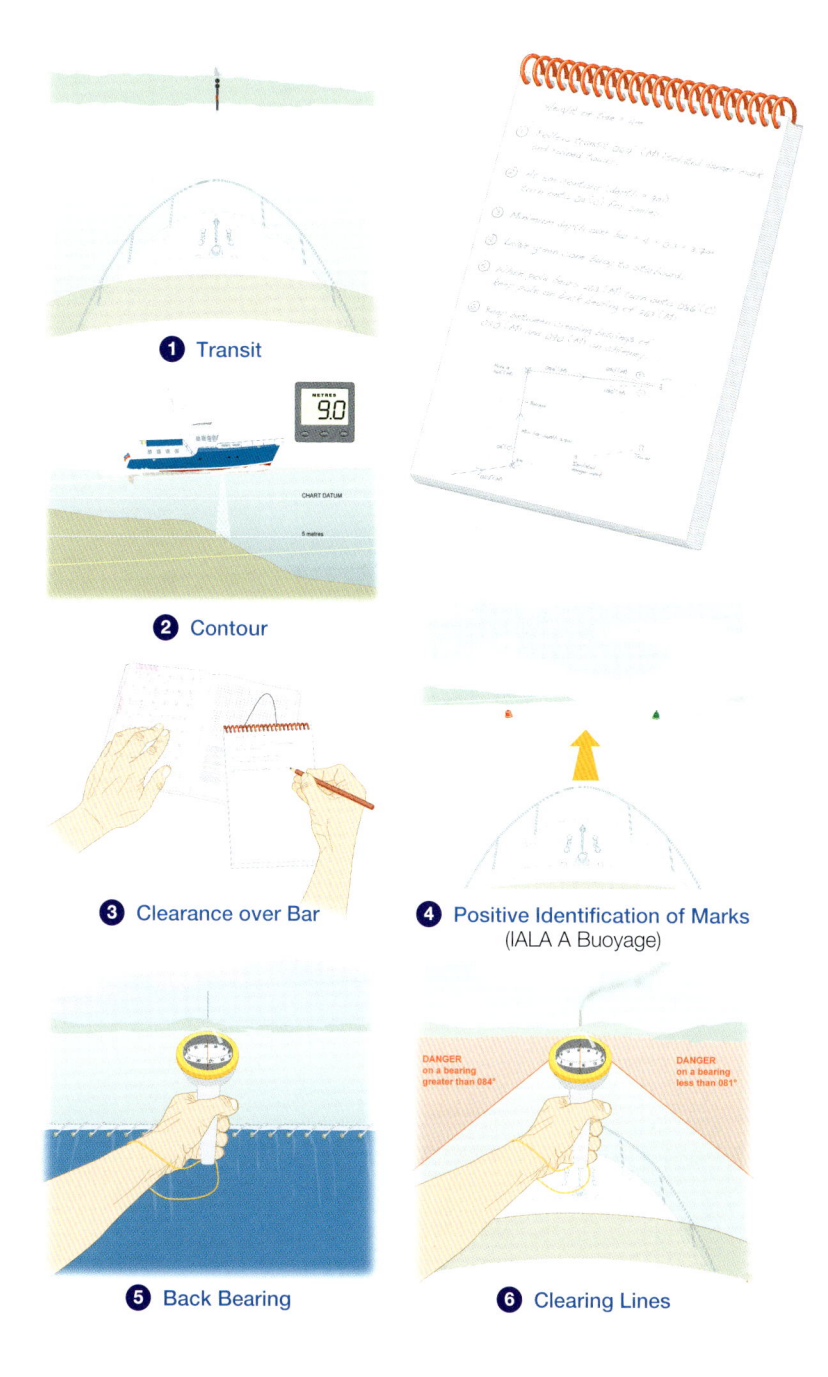

**1** Transit

**2** Contour

**3** Clearance over Bar

**4** Positive Identification of Marks
(IALA A Buoyage)

**5** Back Bearing

**6** Clearing Lines

[ 117 ]

Weather Systems

# Weather Systems

### General Overview

Low- and high-pressure systems dictate our weather. They revolve in different directions, depending on which hemisphere they inhabit. Where you are cruising on the earth's surface will dictate whether lows, highs or a mixture of both dictate your weather. In the UK, low-pressure systems dictate our weather. In many places in the Southern Hemisphere, cold fronts dictate the weather scene.

In the Northern Hemisphere, low-pressure systems revolve anti-clockwise and highs revolve clockwise.

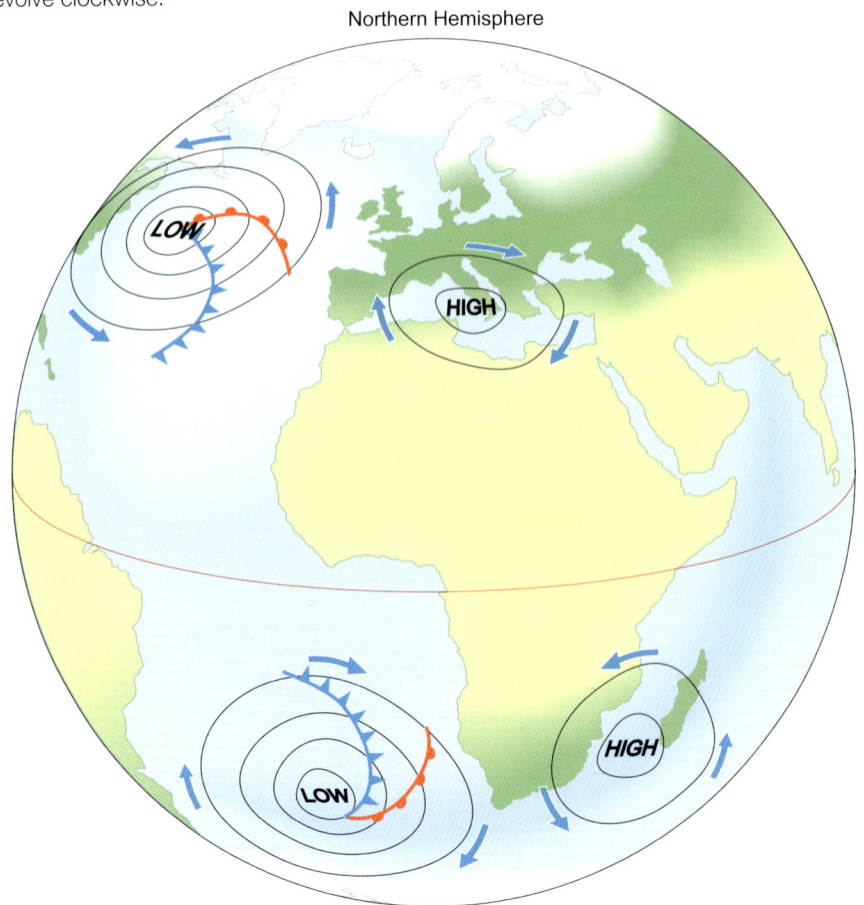

Northern Hemisphere

Southern Hemisphere

In the Southern Hemisphere, low-pressure systems revolve clockwise and highs revolve anticlockwise.

## Weather Systems

### NORTHERN HEMISPHERE

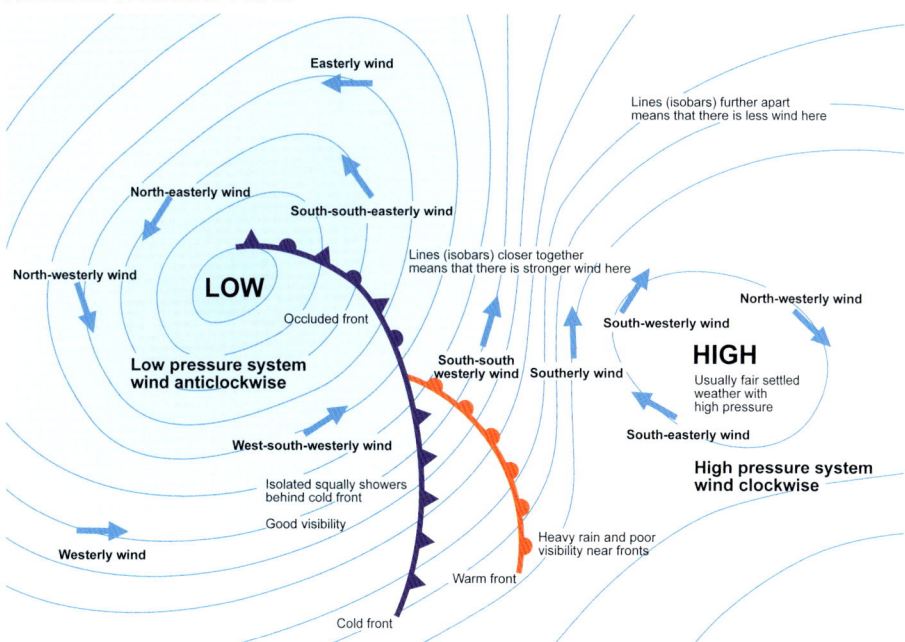

### SOUTHERN HEMISPHERE

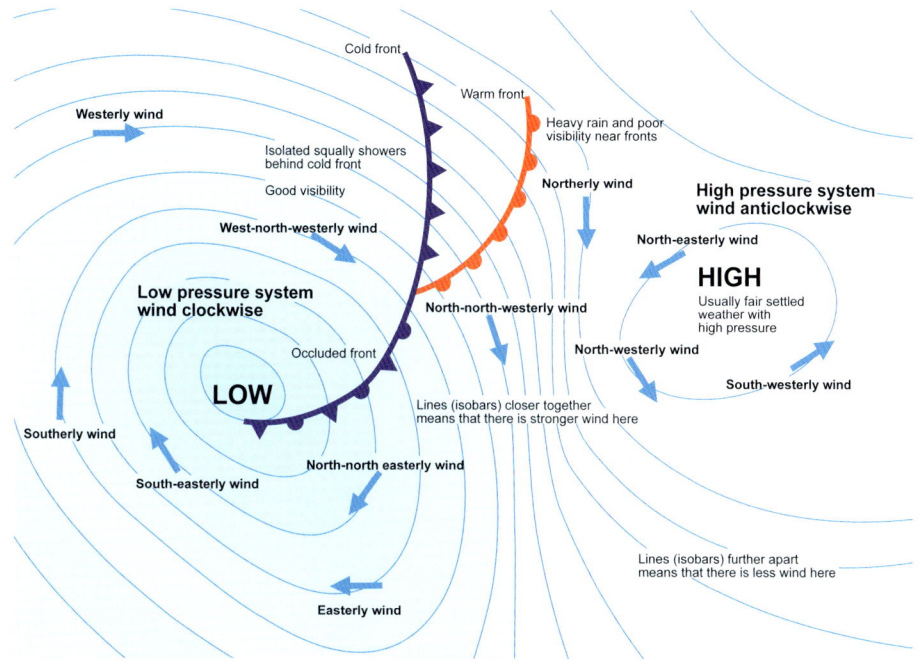

# Weather Forecasts

### Shipping Forecast Areas
Get to know your local forecast area.

There are many different ways to obtain a forecast.

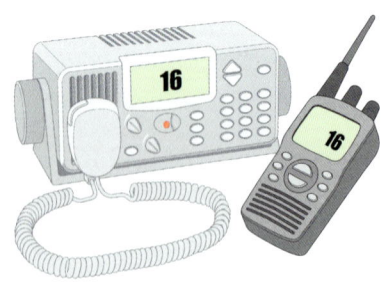

Marine safety information broadcasts on VHF by the Coastguard.

The internet – perhaps for many the easiest answer.

Recorded forecasts by phone.

Many harbour and marina offices post a forecast.

Smartphone apps.

National and local radio stations.

## Weather Forecasts

## TERMS USED IN FORECASTS

| | |
|---|---|
| Gale warnings | If average wind is expected to be F8 or more (34–40 knots), or gusts 43–51 knots.<br>Severe gale: Winds of force 9 (41–47 knots) or gusts reaching 52–60 knots.<br>Storm: Winds of force 10 (48–55 knots) or gusts reaching 61–68 knots.<br>Violent storm: Winds of force 11 (56–63 knots) or gusts of 69 knots or more.<br>Hurricane force: Winds of force 12 (64 knots or more). |
| Strong wind warnings | If average wind is expected to be F6 or F7. F6 is often called a 'yachtsman's gale'. |
| Imminent | Within 6 hours of time of issue of warning. |
| Soon | Within 6–12 hours of time of issue of warning. |
| Later | More than 12 hours from time of issue of warning. |
| Visibility | Good = greater than 5 miles.<br>Moderate = between 2–5 miles.<br>Poor = 1,000m to 2 miles.<br>Very Poor = less than 1,000m. |
| Fair | No significant precipitation. |
| Backing | Wind changing in an anti-clockwise direction e.g. NW to SW. |
| Veering | Wind changing in a clockwise direction e.g. NE to SE. |
| General synopsis | How and where the weather systems are moving. |
| Sea states | Smooth = wave height 0.2–0.5m.<br>Slight = wave height 0.5–1.25m.<br>Moderate = wave height 1.25m–2.5m.<br>Rough = wave height 2.5m–4m.<br>Very rough = wave height 4m–6m.<br>High = wave height 6m–9m.<br>Very high = wave height 9m–14m.<br>Phenomenal = wave height more than 14m. |
| Movement of pressure systems | Slowly = moving at less than 15 knots.<br>Steadily = moving at 15–25 knots.<br>Rather quickly = moving at 25–35 knots.<br>Rapidly = moving at 35–45 knots.<br>Very rapidly = moving at more than 45 knots. |
| Pressure tendency in station reports | Rising (or falling) more slowly = pressure rising (or falling) at a progressively slower rate through the preceding three hours.<br>Rising (or falling) slowly = pressure change of 0.1 to 1.5 hPa in the preceding three hours.<br>Rising (or falling) = pressure change of 1.6 to 3.5 hPa in the preceding three hours.<br>Rising (or falling) quickly = pressure change of 3.6 to 6.0 hPa in the preceding three hours.<br>Rising (or falling) very rapidly = Pressure change of more than 6.0 hPa in the preceding three hours<br>Now rising (or falling) = Pressure has been falling (rising) or steady in the preceding three hours, but at the time of observation was definitely rising (or falling).<br><br>Note: For those more familiar with the millibar, 1 hPa = 1 mbar |

Land and Sea Breezes

# Land and Sea Breezes

## Sea Breeze

In fair weather and light to moderate offshore wind, a sea breeze is likely to develop. Warm air rises over land. It then cools, descends and blows onshore. The wind is up to force 4 in strength.

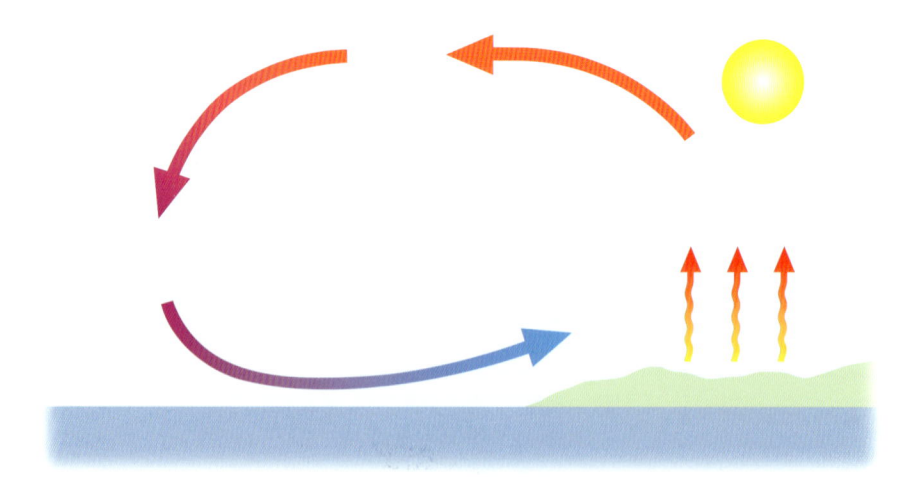

## Land Breeze

This occurs on a clear night when the air cools over land and flows downhill and out to sea, particularly from river estuaries. The wind is usually no more than force 2–3, except near mountains.

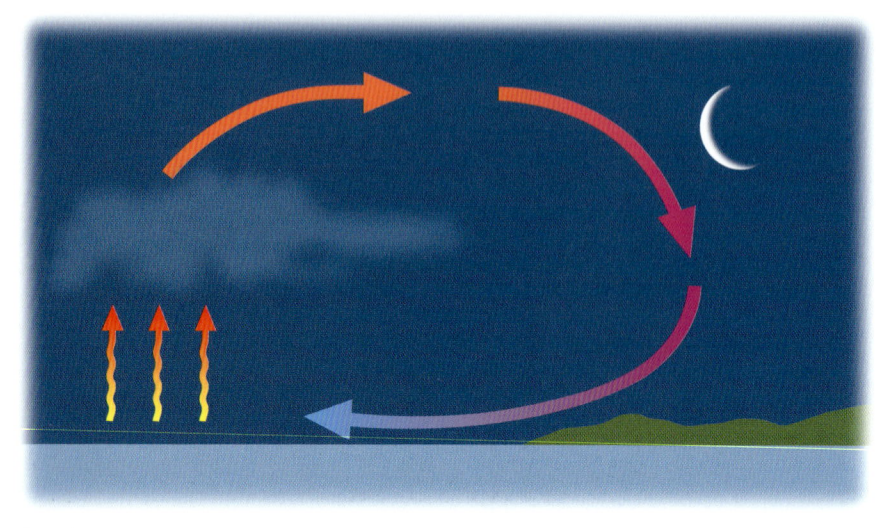

# Weather and Passage Making

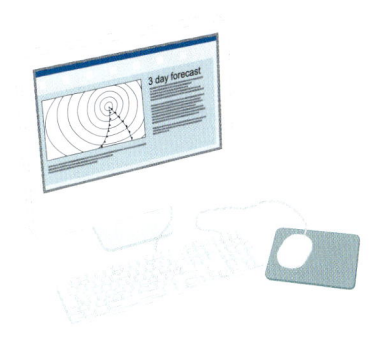

**1** Obtain a forecast.

**2** Look ahead. How will the weather affect you?

**3** How does the wind affect your plan? Be prepared to change your plans.

Outward passage downwind.

Return passage into wind – very uncomfortable.

Make sure you and your crew are prepared for what the weather will bring.

Weather and Passage Making

**4** Wind over tide gives short steep waves.

**5** Calmer conditions can be found in the lee of the land.

**6** Learn to read the water for indications of wind.

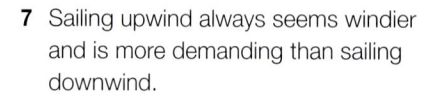

**7** Sailing upwind always seems windier and is more demanding than sailing downwind.

# Beaufort Wind Scale

**F1**      **F3**      **F5**

**F6**      **F8**      **F10**

1. Light airs. 1–3 knots. Ripples. Sail = drifting conditions. Power = fast planing conditions.

2. Light breeze. 4–6 knots. Small wavelets. Sail = full mainsail and large genoa. Power = fast planing conditions.

3. Gentle breeze. 7–10 knots. Occasional crests. Sail = full sail. Power = fast planing conditions.

4. Moderate. 11–16 knots. Frequent white horses. Sail = reduce headsail size. Power = may have to slow down if wind against tide.

5. Fresh breeze. 17–21 knots. Moderate waves, many white crests. Sail = reef mainsail. Power = reduce speed to prevent slamming when going upwind.

6. Strong breeze. 22–27 knots. Large waves, white foam crests. Sail = reef main and reduce headsail. Power = displacement speed.

7. Near gale. 28–33 knots. Sea heaps up, spray, breaking waves, foam blows in streaks. Sail = deep reefed main, small jib. Power = displacement speed.

8. Gale. 34–40 knots. Moderately high waves, breaking crests. Sail = deep reefed main, storm jib. Power = displacement speed, stem waves.

9. Severe gale. 41–47 knots, High waves, spray affects visibility. Sail = trysail and storm jib. Power = displacement speed, stern waves.

10. Storm. 48–55 knots. Very high waves, long breaking crests. Survival conditions.

11. Violent storm. 56–63 knots. Exceptionally high seas with continuously breaking waves seriously affecting visibility. Survival tactics.

12. Hurricane. 64 knots and above. Exceptionally high seas with continuously breaking waves seriously affecting visibility. Survival tactics.

www.rya.org.uk/go/join

# LOVE YACHT CRUISING?
## Then why not join the association that supports you?
### Join the RYA today and benefit from

- Representing your interests and defending your rights of navigation
- Your International Certificate of Competence at no charge
- World leading Yachtmaster™ scheme
- Free sail numbers for Gold Members
- Personal advice and information on a wide range of cruising topics
- Legal advice on buying and selling a boat and other boating related matters
- The latest news delivered to your door or inbox by RYA magazine and e-newsletters
- Boat show privileges including an exclusive free RYA members' lounge
- Discounts on a wide range of products and services including boat insurance

### Get more from your boating; support the RYA

**Want to know more?**
Then call our friendly and helpful membership team on 0844 556 9556 or email: member.services@rya.org.uk

The RYA… be part of it                              www.rya.org.uk

# Shop online at
# www.rya.org.uk/shop

- Secure online ordering
- 15% discount for RYA members
- Books, DVDs, navigation aids and lots more
- Free delivery to a UK address for RYA members on orders over £25
- Free delivery to an overseas address for RYA members on orders over £50
- Buying online from the RYA shop enables the RYA in its work on behalf of its members

# RYA Training Courses
## for all ages, abilities and aspirations

*Get the most from your time on the water with our range of practical and shorebased courses.*

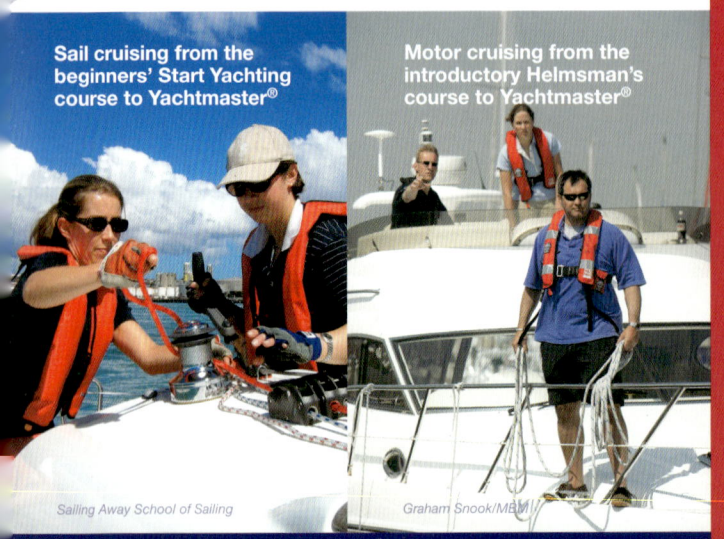

**Sail cruising from the beginners' Start Yachting course to Yachtmaster®**

**Motor cruising from the introductory Helmsman's course to Yachtmaster®**

Sailing Away School of Sailing

Graham Snook/MBM

Also, a whole range of navigation and specialist short courses:

> **ESSENTIAL NAVIGATION AND SEAMANSHIP**
> **DAY SKIPPER**
> **COASTAL SKIPPER/ YACHTMASTER® OFFSHORE**
> **YACHTMASTER® OCEAN**
> **DIESEL ENGINE**
> **OFFSHORE SAFETY**
> **VHF RADIO**
> **RADAR**
> **SEA SURVIVAL**
> **FIRST AID**

**For further information see www.rya.org.uk, call 00 44 (0)23 8060 4158 for a brochure or email training@rya.org.uk**